MARSIGLIO OF PADUA

Writings on the Empire

Defensor minor and *De translatione Imperii*

EDITED BY

CARY J. NEDERMAN

Department of Political Science
University of Arizona
Tucson, Arizona

CAMBRIDGE
UNIVERSITY PRESS

Published by the Press Syndicate of the University of Cambridge
The Pitt Building, Trumpington Street, Cambridge CB2 1RP
40 West 20th Street, New York, NY 10011-4211, USA
10 Stamford Road, Oakleigh, Melbourne 3166, Australia

First published 1993

Printed in Great Britain at the University Press, Cambridge

A catalogue record for this book is available from the British Library

Library of Congress cataloguing in publication data

Marsilius, of Padua, d. 1342?
[Defensor minor. English]
Marsiglio of Padua : writings on the Empire : Defensor minor
and De translations Imperii / edited by Cary J. Nederman.
p.   cm. – (Cambridge texts in the history of political thought)
Includes index.
ISBN 0–521–40277–8. – ISBN 0–521–40846–6 (pbk.)
1. State, The.   2. Church and state.
3. Political science – Early works to 1800.
I. Nederman, Cary J.
II. Marsilius, of Padua, d. 1342.. De translations Imperii. English. 1993.
III. Title.   IV. Title: Writings on the Empire.   V. Series
JC121.M31713   1993
322'.1–dc20   92–33311   CIP

ISBN 0 521 40277 8   hardback
ISBN 0 521 40846 6   paperback

For my students at the University of Canterbury

Contents

Defensor minor

(translated by Cary J. Nederman)

De translatione Imperii

(translated by Fiona Watson and Cary J. Nederman)

Acknowledgements

My interest in the later career of Marsiglio of Padua can be traced to an undergraduate seminar given by Professor Julian Franklin at Columbia University in 1977. Professor Franklin and his colleagues in the Political Science, Philosophy and History Departments at Columbia promoted a standard of scholarship which I have always sought to uphold. More recently, my research on Marsiglio has benefited from the friendly yet critical comments of Professors Neal Wood and Conal Condren and Dr Janet Coleman. My friends Professors Kate Langdon Forhan and Carole Levin lent moral support at critical moments. My partner, Arlen Feldwick, read the entire text, making many valuable suggestions for its improvement. She also created the indices and critical apparatus. The University of Canterbury Minor Research Grant Programme defrayed some of the expenses incurred in preparing the manuscript.

During five years of association with the University of Canterbury, I was fortunate to teach a large number of remarkably gifted and stimulating students, some of whom are now pursuing their own academic careers. I can only mention a few names: Catherine Campbell, Michèle Hollis, Erik Koed, Kirsten Mackay, Martin Morris, Michael Shaw, and Tim Sinclair. These students and their contemporaries often taught me far more than I was able to impart to them. My dedication of this book to them is a small way of acknowledging their special contributions.

Editor's introduction

The reputation of Marsiglio of Padua (sometimes known by the Latinized version of his name, Marsilius) rests almost entirely on his authorship of the *Defensor pacis* ('The Defender of the Peace'). Completed in 1324, the *Defensor pacis* has been an object of curiosity and controversy since its own century, both because it advocates a startlingly secularist concept of the origins and nature of the political community and because of its unwavering opposition to the powers and prerogatives of the church and the papacy as forces in temporal life. The fame of the *Defensor pacis* spread as its doctrines were borrowed by some later medieval authors, even as Marsiglio's teachings were also reviled in strident attacks by orthodox churchmen. When judged according to its innovations as well as its influence, the *Defensor pacis* must be counted in the first rank of contributions to the development of political theory during the Latin Middle Ages.

The *Defensor pacis* has consequently overshadowed Marsiglio's other writings. In addition to several works on metaphysical topics attributed to him, Marsiglio wrote two further political tracts: a recapitulation and synopsis of the main points of the *Defensor pacis*, entitled the *Defensor [pacis] minor*, and an historical survey of the origins and development of the Roman Empire, called *De translatione Imperii* ('On the Transfer of the Empire'). The significance of these political writings is three-fold. First, they extend the doctrines enunciated in the *Defensor pacis* and clarify some of its ambiguities. Second, they permit us to judge the extent to which he refined or altered his theoretical stance in the light of subsequent events and experiences. Third, they afford insight into the political and intellectual climate at the court of German King Ludwig IV of Bavaria, who had lent his protection to some of the most prominent heretics and persecuted figures of early fourteenth-century Europe.

Early life

Born between about 1275 and 1280, Marsiglio was a member of the prominent Mainardini family of Padua. Among Marsiglio's immediate relatives were lawyers, judges and notaries; his father occupied the position of notary of the University of Padua. Because the professional guilds connected with the practice of law exercised great influence over the government of the commune of Padua, Marsiglio was directly exposed to the operation of urban political affairs from a young age. His early life and education is in the main obscure. He was trained as a physician (quite probably at Padua, one of Europe's leading medical schools). He was a friend of Paduan civic leader and noted prehumanist author Albertino Mussato, who, in a famous verse letter addressed to 'Master Marsilius, Paduan physician, censuring him for his fickleness', claims to have encouraged Marsiglio to undertake the study of medicine in preference to law. He was also associated with the powerful della Scalla family of Verona and with Matteo Visconti of Milan, in whose political enterprises he was to be engaged throughout his life.

The first date that may securely be assigned to Marsiglio is 12 March 1313, when a charter of the University of Paris identifies him as Rector of that institution. He would have occupied this position for three months in early 1313. Information about Marsiglio's activities improves thereafter. In 1315, he witnesses a profession of faith by a fellow scholar; in 1316, and again in 1318, he is promised ecclesiastical preferment by Pope John XXII; in 1319, he is mentioned (also in a letter of John XXII) as a member of a diplomatic mission on behalf of della Scalla and Visconti interests. Marsiglio's friend Mussato chides him about his failure to settle on an academic career: 'fleeing from the path of sacred study, you incline towards the disgraceful acts of men'. Indeed, the chief token of Marsiglio's 'fickleness' for Mussato was his attraction to political affairs.

When or where Marsiglio began to compose the *Defensor pacis* is uncertain. At roughly 500 pages in modern critical editions, and with frequent cross references, it seems to have been carefully constructed over a lengthy period of time by an author with access to a considerable library. Moreover, the text of the *Defensor pacis* speaks so often of King

Philip IV (the Fair) of France, and of that ruler's conflicts with Popes Boniface VIII and Clement V, as to suggest the recent memory of these figures. Philip died in 1314. That the *Defensor pacis* may have been started soon after 1315 is suggested by a reference in it to the French Baronial Leagues of 1314–15 as 'modern'. In any case, Marsiglio completed the *Defensor pacis* in Paris on the Feast Day of St John the Baptist (24 June) 1324.

The *Defensor pacis* is composed of three parts or discourses. Discourse I discusses the origins and nature of temporal political authority, concentrating on popular consent as the touchstone of good government without advocating any particular set of constitutional arrangements. The second discourse, nearly four times the length of the first, critically surveys and refutes a variety of claims made on behalf of the earthly power of priests and, especially, the pope, and proposes that the church should be governed by a general council of its members. A third brief discourse summarizes those conclusions derived from the preceding discussions which Marsiglio regards as especially useful or worthy of emphasis. The thematic division between Discourses I and II, implying a distinction between the treatment of temporal government and of ecclesiastical affairs, is unusual for its time. Most of Marsiglio's contemporaries integrated their secular political theory into writings which were primarily concerned with the relation between spiritual and earthly realms.

The *Defensor pacis* initially circulated without any attribution, although clues to its authorship (such as the self-identification of its author as 'a son of Antenor' (the legendary founder of Padua) and a lengthy encomium of Matteo Visconti) abound in the text. Only in 1326, under circumstances which continue to be mysterious, was Marsiglio publicly connected with the *Defensor pacis*. He fled Paris immediately, along with his colleague John of Jandun (who for centuries was erroneously thought to be co-author of the *Defensor pacis*), finding refuge in Nuremberg at the court of the German king, Ludwig, who was in the midst of a longstanding dispute with the papacy over his rights to exercise royal and imperial powers within Germany and Northern Italy.

De translatione Imperii: origins and purpose

One of the papacy's polemical weapons against independently-minded emperors such as Ludwig was a document known as the 'Donation of Constantine'. The 'Donation' purports to be a fourth-century grant of lordship over all the lands within the Empire to the bishop of Rome by the first Christian Emperor, Constantine I. (The Roman bishop then relinquished the day-to-day supervision of the imperial administration back to the emperor.) This document, in turn, became the basis for medieval explanations of how the seat of the Empire was transferred first to the Franks and later to the Germans: it fell to the authority of the papacy, as warranted by the 'Donation', to assign imperial rights to one particular dynasty or people. During the Renaissance, the 'Donation of Constantine' was revealed to be an early medieval forgery, and even in Marsiglio's day there were doubts about its authenticity. Nevertheless, it proved to be powerful ammunition for late medieval popes and the writers who served their cause.

In the *Defensor pacis*, Marsiglio had attempted to refute the conclusions which papal proponents derived from the 'Donation'. In particular, he argued that since the exercise of rulership in any temporal society can stem only from the community itself, or its greater part, no pope or other priest can rightfully invoke his own authority to transfer political power from one person to another or the seat of the Empire from one place to another. Such a position depended directly upon his teachings about the nature of secular politics in Discourse I. Two conclusions were possible on the basis of this argument: first, that the papacy had on its own initiative directed the transfer of the Empire amongst individuals or nations, and hence that all such transfers were illegitimate; or second, that the role of the papacy in successive transfers of the Empire was not decisive, but rather that these transfers in fact occurred in accordance with the principles outlined in the *Defensor pacis* and so were *de iure* as well as *de facto*. Marsiglio says in Discourse II that, while he will assume the latter conclusion to be valid, the legitimacy of the successive imperial transfers needs to be demonstrated, a task which he proposes to undertake in another work, by which he clearly means the text known as *De translatione Imperii*.

De translatione Imperii cannot be dated with great precision. Because it refers to and draws explicitly from a work on the same topic by Landolfo Colonna, which was completed in 1324, it was certainly begun only after the *Defensor pacis* was finished. But whether Marsiglio turned to this project at once, or postponed it, cannot be ascertained. The most likely conjecture is that he wrote the treatise while still in Paris, or at least prior to the death of Pope John XXII in 1334, since John in particular had encouraged the view that the papacy enjoyed an historical authority to transfer the imperial seat, and hence to appoint and depose Emperors.

The purpose of *De translatione Imperii* is two-fold. First, it seeks to establish that the current incumbent of the office of the Roman Emperor holds his position as the result of a series of rightful transfers of power and in accordance with the correct procedure for his selection. Second, it aims to show that no matter how central a role the papacy may have played in facilitating the transfer of the imperial seat to the Franks and later to the Germans, its function was purely honorific and incidental. Thus, even if custom has permitted popes to crown new emperors, the source of imperial authority is not the papacy but an earthly historical process outside of papal control. The challenge for Marsiglio becomes the collection of historical evidence to support his position.

Marsiglio meets the challenge by adapting Landolfo's *Tractatus de translatione Imperii* ('Treatise on the Transfer of the Empire') to suit purposes for which it was not intended. Landolfo had collated the available chronicles and historical literature on the subject in order to vindicate the papal interpretation of its rights over the Empire. By judicious editing and critical reexamination of the sources, Marsiglio's purported summary of Landolfo's work reaches a radically different conclusion. Marsiglio is not engaged in the enterprise of historical writing in a recognizably modern sense; his goals are wholly polemical. Yet his *De translatione Imperii* represents an ingenious attempt to confront the historical claims of papal supporters directly and to dismantle them by means of a sort of immanent critique. History constitutes for Marsiglio still another battlefield – along with the realms of reason and revelation – upon which the pretensions of papal supremacy in the temporal sphere need to be repulsed.

Later career

Marsiglio's public identification as author of the *Defensor pacis*, and subsequent flight from Paris, occasioned a new phase in his career. Cut off from a formal academic environment, he devoted himself to the active promotion of the interests of his protector, Ludwig. The German king had captured his crown in 1322 after a prolonged struggle against another claimant, but Pope John XXII refused to acknowledge his royal and imperial rights and prerogatives. Ludwig's desire for allies in what would prove to be another two decades of (ultimately fruitless) conflict with the papacy explains his readiness to act as patron to Marsiglio and his friend John of Jandun, as well as to a host of other influential fourteenth-century figures, among them the philosopher William of Ockham, the lawyer Bonagratia of Bergamo, the theologian Ubertino de Casale, and Michael of Cesena, the head of the Franciscan order and leader of its so-called 'Spiritual' wing.

That Marsiglio's work was immediately associated with Ludwig's cause by the Roman curia is suggested by the contents of the October 1327 bull *Licit iuxta*, in which John XXII condemns the author of the *Defensor pacis* on the basis of reports of some of its leading ideas. The specific propositions which *Licit iuxta* identifies as heretical indicate much about the motives behind John's condemnation. Five claims are singled out: (1) that Christ, in surrendering tribute to Roman authorities, did so because he was subject to the coercive power of the temporal ruler; (2) that the apostle Peter enjoyed no special authority over the other apostles or the church as a whole; (3) that the emperor can appoint, remove and punish the pope; (4) that all priests, regardless of title or rank, are equal in spiritual authority, so that distinctions within the clergy are entirely a matter of imperial concession; and (5) that the church can punish no person coercively without the grant of the emperor. These assertions all relate directly to the terms of the conflict between Ludwig and John XXII. Marsiglio's book, together with his presence at Ludwig's court, provided further justification for the pope's proclamations that the German king was a heretic.

The expressly political nature of John XXII's motives for the condemnation of the *Defensor pacis* are also suggested by Marsiglio's public role at the time. In early 1327, Ludwig had launched an expedition into the Italian peninsula designed to establish his influence over the *Regnum Italicum*, that is, the provinces of Northern Italy which were traditionally subject to the German Empire. He undertook this journey on the advice of his Italian supporters, including the Visconti and della Scalla families, who counselled that the pope's absence from Rome (the papacy had resided at Avignon under French protection since 1305) enhanced Ludwig's chances of promoting his cause among the cities of Italy. He visited numerous locations in Lombardy during the spring and summer of 1327, where he was uniformly welcomed, and meanwhile continued to engage in diplomatic manoeuvres with the papacy.

The autumn saw Ludwig move southward into central Italy, heading toward Rome, where he arrived on 7 January 1328. Following a meeting of the commune of the city, he was formally invited to enter Rome and on 17 January was crowned Emperor in St Peter's by Sciarra Colonna in the name of the Roman people. Was this part of Ludwig's plan all along, or was it instead the result of his frustration with John XXII's intransigence? The evidence is ambiguous. Even after these events, Ludwig maintained diplomatic efforts to resolve his differences with the papacy, although they were consistently rebuffed. Eventually, however, he deposed his papal adversary and appointed an anti-pope, who took the name Nicholas V.

Scholars have detected the hand of Marsiglio in the course of events during 1327 and 1328. Marsiglio entered Italy with Ludwig's entourage, although he was not constantly at the side of the German king. For instance, Marsiglio was present in Milan during November 1327, when Ludwig was in the vicinity of Lucca. Ludwig appointed Marsiglio 'spiritual vicar' of Rome, in which capacity he seems to have drafted a number of documents associated with his patron's residence in that city. Certainly, many of the formal and rhetorical features of Ludwig's Roman adventure bear a Marsiglian stamp. But the true extent of Marsiglio's role in designing the scenario remains unresolved.

Ludwig's triumph was short-lived. During the spring of 1328, the papacy augmented its efforts to remove the German presence from Rome, Italian opponents of the king began to marshal their forces, and the Roman populace grew disenchanted. Ludwig withdrew from the city on 4 August 1328, and retraced his steps through Italy until he reached the Alpine city of Trent in the following December. There he once again sought the counsel of his Italian supporters, reaffirmed the deposition of John XXII, and retired to Germany. Marsiglio was positively identified by a contemporary source as one of the members of Ludwig's retreating procession.

After his return to Germany Marsiglio's activities become obscure. His name is occasionally mentioned in correspondence between Ludwig and the papacy, but there is no evidence of any literary production during the next decade. Ludwig's cause was instead pressed in writing by William of Ockham, Michael of Cesena and other exiled churchmen and intellectuals at the imperial court. It is generally assumed that Marsiglio spent the 1330s practising medicine; it has been surmised that he fell out of favour with Ludwig and was perhaps banished from the circle of royal associates and advisors. Whatever his situation in the intervening years, Marsiglio did return to polemical pursuits briefly at the end of his life.

(Because of a passing reference in a document of Pope Clement VI, it is known that Marsiglio was dead by April 1343, and most probably died in late 1342.) The outcome of this final spurt of activity was the *Defensor minor*.

Defensor minor: circumstances of composition

Following the failure of his Italian expedition, King Ludwig eschewed further direct action and concentrated instead upon a diplomatic solution to his conflict with the papacy. He sent envoys on a regular basis to negotiate with John XXII and, after John's death, with his successor Benedict XII. Ludwig's instructions to his ambassadors throughout this period suggest an essential pragmatism and flexibility: he was prepared to recognize the papal right to approve the incumbent of the papal office and to submit to penance for offending the papacy by his conduct during the Italian expedition, but he would not concede any prerogatives (especially in regard to Italy) that might harm his material interests. His concerns centred upon tangible benefits and costs rather than symbolism.

Ludwig's policies augured poorly for Marsiglio, whose opposition to the papacy rested on intractable points of principle. More popular at Ludwig's court were William of Ockham and others who advocated a more moderate position towards the pope. In written instructions given to his emissaries to Avignon in 1331, and again in 1336, Ludwig volunteered to withdraw protection from Marsiglio should the king's servant not follow his master in the terms of some future reconciliation with the pope. Marsiglio's intransigence made him a liability in the context of delicate diplomacy.

For a time, Ludwig's diplomatic approach promised to bear fruit. Benedict XII, although he laid down strict prerequisites for the legitimation of the Bavarian claim to the crown, appeared more pliant than his predecessor, and by early 1337, it seemed that the gulf between the parties would be bridged. But a French desire to thwart any agreement, combined with lingering distrust of Ludwig's readiness to honour his promises, produced a breakdown in discussions. Never again, despite the concerted efforts of the royal ambassadors, would a reconciliation between king and papacy be so close.

These events may have lent weight to Marsiglio's assertion that any compromise with the papacy was not only untenable but futile, and hence encouraged him to take up the pen once again. But a more immediate stimulus was a request from his patron for an opinion regarding the propriety of the divorce of Margaret Maultasch, Countess of Tyrol and Carinthia, and her proposed wedding to Ludwig's son, Ludwig of Brandenberg. Margaret had been married in 1330, when twelve years of age, to the ten-year-old Prince John Henry of Bohemia, a union which had allegedly never been consummated and of which she sought a dissolution in 1340. Ludwig's plan was to wed Margaret to his own offspring, thereby bringing Tyrol under his direct control. This second marriage, too, was problematic, for Margaret's grandmother and Ludwig's grandfather had been siblings, thus raising questions about the consanguinity of the prospective partners. Ordinarily, the procedure for effecting such a marriage would involve seeking the permission of the pope for the annulment of Margaret's first marriage and his dispensation for her to wed a blood relation. But Ludwig's standing with the papacy, and the interdict which had been placed on him and his associates, precluded this route.

Ludwig thus posed the question: must the pope (or any clergyman) approve the dissolution of a marriage and/or the betrothal of persons related by blood? Both Marsiglio and William of Ockham seem to have been consulted about this matter; William produced a work entitled *Consultatio de causa matrimoniali* ('Consultation regarding the Marriage Case'), which has been dated to 1341. Marsiglio contributed three separate tracts: a brief exemplar for Ludwig's proclamation of Margaret's divorce (*Forma divorcii matrimonalis* or 'Form of the Dissolution of Marriage'); a much longer discussion of the essentially secular nature of the marital bond (*De matrimonio*); and a model for the imperial declaration of the legitimacy of marriage between individuals related by blood (*Forma dispensationis super affinitatem consanguinitatis*). The body of *De matrimonio* is substantially the same as chapters 13–15 of the *Defensor minor*, while chapter 16 is an adaptation of *Forma dispensationis*. These would have been completed prior to 10 February 1342, when Ludwig's plans for Margaret were realized in the celebration of her marriage to the younger Ludwig; they might even have been finished by November 1341, when John Henry was expelled from the Countess' household. That Marsiglio was asked for advice in this matter at all is perhaps the clearest indication that, whatever his status during the 1330s, he commanded the respect of the German court in 1340.

A third factor shaping Marsiglio's later literary production was no doubt the numerous attacks and critiques which the *Defensor pacis* had spawned. From the late 1320s onwards, papalists repeatedly condemned the heretical features of his thought, concentrating on the refutation of his denial of a papal plenitude of power. Moreover, later authors had attempted to refine and restate the grounds for papal claims to authority in temporal affairs, and thus to undermine indirectly Marsiglio's arguments. Finally, his work had also been challenged by fellow supporters of the imperial cause, especially William of Ockham, who openly disputed Marsiglian doctrines in writings which probably date from the late 1330s and early 1340s. That Marsiglio was aware of the extent and range of the polemics directed against the *Defensor pacis* is evident from the *Defensor minor*, where he recurrently responds to 'certain people' who have adopted positions at variance with his own. The *Defensor minor* constitutes a sort of 'reply to critics' and reaffirmation of the principles contained in the *Defensor pacis*.

Except for his opinions about the divorce and remarriage of Margaret, one cannot date the text of the *Defensor minor* with any great precision. Since the sections on the Maultasch affair must have been composed between 1340 and the very beginning of 1342, the essential question about the rest of the *Defensor minor* is: did Marsiglio write it before he was consulted about the proposed divorce and marriage (in which case, chapters 13–16 were appended to an already completed work), or afterwards? Scholarship is divided over the answer. Some have argued that the first twelve chapters were composed in 1342, as a sort of explanation of and framework for the Maultasch opinions. But the weight of evidence points to 1339–40 as the most likely years for the composition of chapters 1–12, although parts of this section might have been drafted even earlier. The discussions of divorce and consanguinity seem to be independent of the main body of the *Defensor minor*. Perhaps after Margaret's marriage Marsiglio conceived the idea of weaving all the materials together. This would account plausibly for the level of repetition between chapters 1–12 and 13–16 and for the generally poor integration of the final four chapters into the overall argument of the treatise. The *Defensor minor* is thus most reliably dated to the period between 1339 and 1342.

Defensor minor: structure and purpose

The *Defensor minor* is, structurally speaking, a more conventionally medieval work than the *Defensor pacis*, in the sense that it does not introduce a cleavage between its discussion of temporal government, on the one hand, and ecclesiology, on the other, and, by inference, between the natural and supernatural realms or between reason and revelation. Rather, Marsiglio's later work concentrates upon the relationship between earthly jurisdiction and spiritual authority. This places the *Defensor minor* squarely within the standard genre of 'king and pope' or 'emperor and pope' treatises typical of the thirteenth and fourteenth centuries.

That Marsiglio focusses in the *Defensor minor* upon the Empire does not signal, however, a reorientation or departure from the *Defensor pacis*. The *Defensor pacis* had adopted a 'generic' approach to the political community, explicitly declining to privilege any constitutional system or geographical unit of association. The *Defensor minor* attempts to translate these general principles of temporal politics into the concrete terms of an imperial regime, in contrast to a city or 'national' kingdom. Marsiglio contends that the Roman Empire, just like any other earthly polity, has an independent foundation stemming from the consent of its corporate community (or 'human legislator'). The papacy enjoys no greater right to interfere in the affairs of the Empire than in any other form of political association.

Consequently, many of the characteristic doctrines of the *Defensor pacis* are reencountered in the *Defensor minor*. Yet the *Defensor minor* also occasionally explores novel themes. For instance, in chapter 7 Marsiglio addresses the claim of priests to be able to exact a price, in the form either of monetary payment or of good works such as pilgrimages or crusading, in return for a diminution or remission of punishment in the after-life. This power, known as the granting of indulgence, is rejected by Marsiglio as beyond the authority of the priesthood: a priest may, through his prayers, ask for clemency from God, but he cannot guarantee that God will heed him. At best, to profess faith by seeking to earn indulgence is comparable with offering confession and asking for the assignment of penance: all of these are 'counsels', that is, optional acts which divine law encourages but does not require of believers. The person who confesses, performs penance or merits indulgence grows in spiritual worth before God's eyes; yet someone who declines to engage in these activities does not thereby violate any divine commandment.

Also new to the *Defensor minor* is a lengthy discussion (in chapters 8 and 9) of whether vows or oaths may be absolved by ecclesiastical authorities. Since vows are sworn to God or a saint, the right was claimed for popes or other priests to excuse individuals from their oaths. Marsiglio recognizes how destructive it would be to political and social order if bonds like oaths of fealty or sworn pledges could be erased or ignored at the command of a clergyman. Thus, he argues that so long as an unconditional vow has been freely and legitimately undertaken, and does not prove to be detrimental in some unforeseen way, the swearer cannot be absolved by anyone – even the pope – of his obligation. Moreover, those who refuse to perform what they have sworn are necessarily subject to divine retribution and may additionally be punished by the temporal community for utilitarian reasons, since their acts are destructive of public order.

The novel concerns of the *Defensor minor* stem primarily from conditions in Germany after the papal interdiction of Ludwig and his supporters in 1322. Technically, anyone who came into contact with the royal court was included in the interdict; such a person could not partake of the sacraments, offer confession or receive absolution, and hence could not be saved. Moreover, oaths sworn to a person under interdict were invalid and their requirements were not to be performed; the papacy in effect reserved for itself the authority to free people from otherwise legitimate vows. It seems doubtful that these consequences of Ludwig's excommunication and anathematization ever seriously impeded the everyday operation of his government. But in Marsiglio's mind they constituted pernicious obstacles to the maintenance of temporal order and required eradication in principle lest they be used by priests and laymen as justification for resistance to the rule of Ludwig.

From *Defensor pacis* to *Defensor minor*

Because the *Defensor minor* operates at a level of greater specificity than the *Defensor pacis*, it erases many of the ambiguities of the earlier work and affords further insight into Marsiglio's fundamental intellectual and political commitments. His use of sources offers one example of an interpretive problem which the *Defensor minor* helps to resolve. In Discourse I of the *Defensor pacis*, Marsiglio relies heavily upon citations from Aristotle's *Politics, Ethics* and other works in order to authorize his theory of the temporal community and its rulership, while the anti-papal arguments contained in the second discourse are profoundly indebted to the terms in which the 'Spiritual' wing of the Franciscan Order couched its dispute with Pope John XXII over the issue of clerical poverty. Yet scholars have for many reasons suspected the sincerity or depth of Marsiglio's dedication to either Aristotelianism or the Spiritual Franciscan cause.

This suspicion is confirmed by the text of the *Defensor minor*, where the authorities cited are mainly biblical, with occasional reliance upon the Fathers (Chrysostom, Augustine, Ambrose) and more rarely still upon medieval sources (Peter Lombard, Hugh of St Victor, Bernard of Clairvaux). Marsiglio's inattention to Aristotelian and Spiritual Franciscan teachings may be explained by his polemical purposes. Just as the *Defensor pacis* was designed to appeal to a cross-section of European political units, so equally it sought to rally proponents of differing intellectual orientations to the anti-papal cause. Marsiglio cloaked the doctrines of the first discourse in Aristotelian garb in order to attract fellow schoolmen by demonstrating that opposition to the papacy was an inescapable consequence of Aristotle's teachings. He connected his thought to the arguments of the Spiritual Franciscans, who afforded the most potent source of opposition to the papacy within the early fourteenth-century church, in order to show how their views led inevitably to his own. In effect, the *Defensor pacis* set out to colonize Aristotelian scholasticism and Spiritual Franciscanism in the name of anti-papalism. In the *Defensor minor*, however, Marsiglio's audience has changed. The appeal to authoritative sources in the *Defensor pacis* turns out to be a further instance of the elastic quality of his thought.

At the same time, the *Defensor minor* also assists in the identification and clarification of the stable elements within Marsiglio's thought. One of the most controversial and ill-defined aspects of the *Defensor pacis* was the exact composition of the 'human legislator' or 'people' or 'civic body', that is, the original, supreme and final authority within the political community. At times, the *Defensor pacis* seems to adopt a highly inclusive conception of citizenship (at least when judged by late medieval standards) which grants equal political standing to all free male adults regardless of social or economic status. Commentators have sometimes attempted to diminish or deny the implications of such a broad definition of entitlement to full civic rights through the citation of apparently mitigating or countervailing passages. But the second chapter of the *Defensor minor* leaves no doubt about Marsiglio's confidence in the competence of ordinary persons to exercise the responsibilities associated with citizenship. Referring to his own comments in the first discourse of the *Defensor pacis*, he asserts that the correction of negligent or harmful rulers pertains to the human legislator, which he then defines with reference to 'workmen' (*fabris*), 'craftsmen' and 'other mechanics' as well as men of prudence or learning. In fact, he declares that if correction has to be undertaken by any single segment of the civic body, rather than the whole, it is preferable to assign this task to the labouring part. This confirms his intention in the *Defensor pacis* to uphold that all citizens, regardless of their station in life, enjoy sufficient powers of reason to judge for themselves whether laws or rulers serve the common good.

The *Defensor minor* also explicates with greater precision Marsiglio's view about the foundations of law. Like the *Defensor minor*, the *Defensor pacis* argues that there are two basic kinds of law: divine law, ordained by God who, along with His son, judges in accordance with it; and human law, established by the human legislator and imposed by those persons to whom the legislator assigns the judicial role. Because Marsiglio insists in the *Defensor pacis* that no human law merits obedience which has not first been expressly authorized by the earthly legislator, he has sometimes been understood to advocate the idea of 'legal positivism', that is, the notion that the essential ingredient in the legitimacy of a statute is its *de facto* enactment by the state. In chapter 8 of the *Defensor minor*, however, he proclaims that human and divine laws should be consistent and mutually reinforcing: God-given law decrees obedience to all human legislation which is not incompatible within divine dictates; human law must promulgate nothing which conflicts with God's will. He adds in chapter 13 that, should a case arise in which some human statute commands what is opposed to divine law, the latter takes absolute precedence over the former. Marsiglio thus embraces a version of the traditional Christian doctrine that all duly ordained human power must be obeyed unless its commands conflict with God's law, at which time the Christian must refuse to submit. But he denies one prominent feature of this doctrine: it is not for priests or prelates to decree such resistance – in as much as they may only advise but never command – but for the individual believer to decide. In turn, since human law is propounded by the whole civic community, it seems unlikely that such conflicts of divine with temporal law will emerge in the first place, since the earthly legislator is coextensive with the body of the faithful.

Finally, the *Defensor minor* permits a more thorough appreciation of the nature and operation of the general council of the church. According to the *Defensor pacis*, the purpose of such a council is the canonical interpretation of Holy Scripture. Although the members of this council are elected by the church as a whole, Marsiglio does not construe it as a representative body in a modern, political sense. Rather, since the truths of scripture are fixed for all time, the council's duty is solely to discover and articulate such truths with reference to the Holy Spirit instead of an earthly constituency. In this sense, the general council is infallible in a way that individual priests or prelates, or their various groupings, cannot be; the council alone has access to eternal truth. During the 1330s, William of Ockham had launched a stinging attack on this doctrine of conciliar infallibility by claiming that since individual members of the council were not capable of unerring insight into God's wisdom, then neither could the council as a whole know unequivocally what is true. Ockham appeared to regard the Marsiglian view as unvarnished mysticism. Marsiglio responds in the twelfth chapter of the *Defensor minor*. He points out that what cannot be accomplished by one person may often be achieved by the cooperation of many. In the case of a general council, this cooperation occurs as the result of discussion and mutual education, by means of which a consensus about the truth is eventually attained. The Holy Spirit is infused in individual members of the council as a result of their reciprocal interaction, through a process similar to that described in the *Defensor pacis* by which civil communities reach agreement about legislation.

Although the *Defensor minor* provides an excellent guide to the doctrines of the *Defensor pacis*, it still deserves to be treated as a coherent work of political thought in its own right. It proceeds from an independent premise: that the division of law, and therefore jurisdiction, between divine and human sources leaves no grounds on which the priesthood or its leaders can legitimately arrogate powers of coercive judgement. Priests are comparable for Marsiglio with physicians and learned men: they are authorized to instruct and counsel, but they may never compel. Marsiglio sketches in the *Defensor minor* a fully integrated conception of the temporal realms of politics, and of the place of religion and the clergy within it, which, if somewhat less detailed than the *Defensor pacis*, achieves a level of precision and clarity which was precluded by the 'generic' character of the earlier work. The *Defensor minor* is more than a derivative adjunct to the *Defensor pacis*; it is a mature and advanced statement of the leading principles of Marsiglian political theory.

Note on texts and translations

This volume marks the first appearance in print of English-language translations of Marsiglio of Padua's *Defensor minor* and *De translatione Imperii*. It seems certain that the latter work was chronologically prior to the former (see the 'Editor's introduction'). However, the order of presentation in the current edition (as in the recent critical edition of Marsiglio's *Oeuvres Mineures* by Colette Jeudy and Jeannine Quillet (Paris, 1979)) has been reversed, since the full significance of the historical narrative in *De translatione Imperii* is only evident to the reader who has first grasped the leading principles of Marsiglio's political thought, which are summarized in the *Defensor minor*.

The text of the *Defensor minor* was initially identified by scholars at the end of the nineteenth century. It has been edited twice, first by C. K. Brampton (Birmingham, 1922), then by Jeudy and Quillet as cited above. This translation is based upon the latter edition, although Brampton's notes have occasionally been consulted. Jeudy and Quillet also include an excellent French translation, and their readings have proved useful in clarifying renderings into English.

Although first printed in the sixteenth century, *De translatione Imperii* appeared in a critical text only in the Jeudy and Quillet volume. The present translation follows this edition. Ms Watson, a research student at the University of Canterbury, produced an initial English version, which Dr Nederman later revised.

Bibliographical note

The best general treatments of medieval philosophy and political thought are:
Antony Black, *Political Thought in Europe, 1250–1450* (Cambridge, 1992).
J. H. Burns, ed., *The Cambridge History of Medieval Political Thought* (Cambridge, 1988).
Norman Kretzmann, Antony Kenny and Jan Pinborg, eds., *The Cambridge History of Later Medieval Philosophy* (Cambridge, 1982).

On Marsiglio's social, political and intellectual background, the following studies are recommended:
C. K. Brampton, 'Ockham, Bonagratia and the Emperor Lewis IV', *Medium Aevum*, 81 (1962), 81–7.
J. R. Hale, J. R. L. Highfield and B. Smalley, eds., *Europe in the Later Middle Ages* (London, 1965).
J. K. Hyde, *Padua in the Age of Dante* (Manchester, 1966).
Society and Politics in Medieval Italy (London, 1973).
Gordon Leff, *Paris and Oxford Universities in the Thirteenth and Fourteenth Centuries* (New York, 1975).
H. S. Offler, 'Empire and Papacy: The Last Struggle', *Transactions of the Royal Historical Society*, Series 5, VI (1956), 21–47.

For treatments of Marsiglio's life and his ideas, see:
Marino Damiata, *Plenitudo Potestatis e Universitas Civium in Marsilio da Padova* (Florence, 1983).
Alan Gewirth, *Marsilius of Padua and Medieval Political Philosophy* (New York, 1951).
Carlo Pincin, *Marsilio* (Turin, 1967).
C. W. Previté-Orton, *Marsilius of Padua* (London, 1935).
Friedrich Prinz, 'Marsilius von Padua', *Zeitschrift für Bayerische Landesgeschichte*, 39 (1976), 39–77.
Jeannine Quillet, *Le Philosophie Politique de Marsile de Padoue* (Paris, 1970).
Nicolai Rubinstein, 'Marsilius of Padua and Italian Political Thought of His Time', in Hale, Highfield and Smalley, eds., *Europe in the Later Middle Ages.*

The range of specialized Marsiglian scholarship is well represented by the proceedings of the 1979 conference on Marsiglio held at Padua, published as volumes 5 (1979) and 6 (1980) of the journal *Medioevo*. See also:

Conal Condren, 'Marsilius of Padua's Argument from Authority', *Political Theory*, 5 (1977), 205–18.

    'Democracy and the *Defensor pacis*: On the English Language Tradition of Marsilian Interpretation', *Il Pensiero Politico*, 13 (1980), 301–16.

Georges de Lagarde, *La Naissance de l'esprit laique au decline du Moyen-Age*, new edition, vol. III: *Le Defensor Pacis* (Louvan and Paris, 1970).

Cary J. Nederman, 'Nature, Justice and Duty in the *Defensor pacis*: Marsiglio of Padua's Ciceronian Impulse', *Political Theory*, 18 (1990), 615–37.

    'Private Will, Public Justice: Household, Community and Consent in Marsiglio of Padua's *Defensor pacis*', *Western Political Quarterly*, 43 (1990), 699–717.

    'Knowledge, Consent and the Critique of Political Representation in Marsiglio of Padua's *Defensor pacis*', *Political Studies*, 39 (1991), 19–35.

Piero di Vona, *I Principi del Defensor Pacis* (Naples, 1974).

Michael Wilks, 'Corporation and Representation in the *Defensor pacis*', *Studia Gratiana*, 15 (1972), 251–92.

Studies focussed on Marsiglio's writings about the Empire are less common. The best discussions are:

C. K. Brampton, 'Introduction', *The Defensor Minor of Marsilius of Padua* (Birmingham, 1922).

Carlo Dolcini, 'Osservazioni sul Defensor Minor di Marsilio da Padova', *Atti della Accademia delle Scienze dell'Istituto di Bologna*, 64 (1975/6), 87–102.

    Marsilo e Ockham (Bologna, 1981).

Colette Jeudy, 'Signes de fin de ligne et traditione: le "De translatione Romani Imperii" de Marsile de Padoue', *Scriptorium*, 27 (1973), 252–62 and plates 15–16.

Colette Jeudy and Jeannine Quillet, 'Introduction generale', '*Defensor minor*: Introduction generale', and '*De translatione Imperii*: Introduction', *Marsile de Padoue: Oeuvres Mineures* (Paris, 1979).

Roberto Lombertini, 'Ockham and Marsilius on an Ecclesiological Fallacy', *Franciscan Studies*, 46 (1986), 301–15.

Principal events in the life of Marsiglio of Padua

c. 1275–80	Born at Padua
1313	Rector of the University of Paris
1316	Appointed canon of Padua (October)
1318	Promised first vacant benefice in Padua by Pope John XXII (April)
1319	Served as emissary of Can Grande della Scalla and Matteo Visconti to Count Charles of La Marche
1324	Finished *Defensor pacis* (24 June)
1324–6(?)	Composed *De translatione Imperii*
1326	Fled Paris for Nuremberg with John of Jandun (spring)
1327	Ludwig IV of Bavaria's expedition to Italy; John XXII's bull *Licit iuxta* condemning Marsiglio as author of the *Defensor pacis* (23 October)
1328	Ludwig crowned Roman Emperor in Rome (17 January); Marsiglio appointed spiritual vicar of Rome; Ludwig's withdrawal from Rome (4 August)
1329	Ludwig returns to Germany (December)
1339–40(?)	Composed chapters 1–12 of the *Defensor minor*
1340–1	Wrote *De matrimonio* and *Forma dispensationis super affinitatem consanguinitatis* (*Defensor minor*, chapters 13–16)
1343	Death reported in *collatio* of Pope Clement VI (10 April)

Defensor minor

(translated by Cary J. Nederman)

The beginning of the book entitled *Defensor minor*, edited by Master Marsiglio of Padua after the *Defensor pacis major*.

Chapter 1

[1] We have previously read in earlier works, according to the claims of the Master of the 'Sentences' [Peter Lombard], that priests have a certain power of binding and also of loosing, namely, of excommunicating sinners and cutting them off from spiritual as well as civil or temporal association [*communicatio*] and from fellowship with others of the faithful – powers which they call 'jurisdiction'. It seems at least appropriate to examine what this jurisdiction is and how many types of it may be identified, and whether, according to any sense of the term, the jurisdiction of the emperor is due to bishops or priests.

[2] Just as the word indicates, therefore, 'jurisdiction' is the pronouncement of right [*dictio iuris*]; moreover, right is the same as law. Indeed, law is two-fold: it is sometimes divine, sometimes human. And taking law in its ultimate and proper meaning, as is written in *Defensor pacis*, Discourse I, chapter 10, divine law is the immediate precept of God without human deliberation regarding voluntary human acts committed or omitted in the present world towards the best end or condition in the future world which human beings are suited to pursue. These are coercive precepts, I say, for transgressors in this world, under

punishment or torment to be carried out in the future rather than the present world. This law is called an immediate precept of God without human deliberation because, although divine law has been promulgated by man (that is, by the apostles and evangelists), still this was not done by them nor by their deliberation, as by an immediate efficient cause, but by them as instruments of God or Christ who is God, as though He were the immediate efficient cause of their movements in this regard. Hence, James 4[:12] says, 'There is a single legislator and judge, He who can condemn and deliver'; and II Peter 1[:21] says, 'No prophecy is asserted by the human spirit, but men who speak the holy words of God are inspired by the Holy Spirit'.

[3] In addition, a compatible and more thorough treatment of such a definition can and should be derived from *Defensor pacis*, Discourse I, chapter 10 and Discourse II, chapters 4, 5, 8 and 9.

[4] By contrast, human law is a precept of the community of citizens [*universitas civium*], or of its greater part [*valentior pars*]; the laws themselves ought to be made by immediate deliberation about any voluntary human acts committed or omitted in the present world towards the best end or condition which any man is suited to pursue in this world. These are coercive precepts, I say, for transgressors in this world under threat of punishment or torment to be carried out against the very same transgressors, as is disclosed in *Defensor pacis*, Discourse I, chapter 10.

[5] On the other hand, the pronouncement of right or law, in so far as it serves present purposes, may be approached in four ways: first, ascertaining the standards or rules for civil actions; second, pronouncing or explaining them to other people; third, promulgating them in the manner of coercive precepts, just as has been stated, which are without exception binding upon all who make and are subject to the laws; and fourth, pronouncing law may be approached by means of specific coercive sanctions against each and every transgressor himself. Now, the first way of pronouncing law pertains to the prudent men [*prudentes*] who devise them; the second way, to learned teachers [*doctores*] or those having authority to teach about them; the third and fourth ways, to those who have the primary and proper authority without qualification to coerce transgressors, which is identical with the authority of the legislator itself; the fourth way of pronouncing the right or law pertains more properly to the judge or ruler speaking with the authority of the legislator, since the power to coerce transgressors is not his own without qualification but is given to him by others and is potentially revocable by the same people.

[6] Therefore, having now set out this preface, we may draw some conclusions from it. The first is that no human beings – communally or separately, cleric or layman – in so far as they are human can or ought to pronounce divine law in the first, third or fourth sense; and one can and ought to grasp the same point with the utmost certainty from *Defensor pacis*, Discourse II, chapters 4, 5, 8 and 9, and from the aforementioned authority of James and Peter. From this it also follows by necessity that no human being, regardless of the preeminence of the status or station which he occupies, has the power or authority to dispense, change, increase or diminish any of the precepts of divine law or to introduce precepts touching upon divine law (in a positive as well as a negative way) which one may detect to be contrary or contradictory to the Scriptures. From this it also follows by even greater necessity that if every or any vow is always to be in compliance with the precepts of divine law, and if, furthermore, marriage between certain degrees of blood relations is prohibited by the aforementioned law, then by no means can any bishop or priest, even the Roman bishop who is called pope, dispense an exemption contrary or contradictory to divine law.

[7] The second conclusion is that the pronouncement of human law in accordance with the proper meaning of law (about which we spoke earlier) established by the third and fourth senses of law does not pertain to any bishop, priest or deacon, or cleric or ecclesiastical minister, regardless of the name by which he is called, either alone or in their single assembly, whether communally or separately; and this can and should be grasped from *Defensor pacis*, Discourse I, chapters 12 and 13 and Discourse II, chapters 4, 5, 8 and 9. For this reason, it follows by necessity that none of the aforementioned ecclesiastical ministers, as enumerated above, has the authority to give dispensation from or relax anything contrary to the precepts or prohibitions of human law. Rather, such dispensations or relaxations are to belong to the Roman ruler, in so far as he is the human legislator, and to his authority alone. From this it follows by necessity that no decretal or decretum of the Roman pontiff or any other priest or deacon whatsoever, or aforementioned minister, or their single assembly, acting on his or its own authority, and not from that given by others, may constitute or ordain law according to the proper and ultimate meaning of law, since it would be neither divine nor human law, as should and can be seen from the preceding chapter; and that no one who transgresses either can or ought to be constrained by punishment or torment of their property or persons from such ecclesiastical

3

ministers. From this it also necessarily follows that neither does the Roman bishop or any aforementioned ecclesiastical minister have jurisdiction nor does he have coercive power in this world over either clerics or laymen, even manifest heretics, unless this jurisdiction should have been conceded by a human legislator, by whom it is potentially revocable whenever it seems to the aforementioned legislator to be expedient: and one can and should grasp this with certainty from the preceding chapter and the *Defensor pacis*, Discourse II, chapter 10. For this reason it also follows that neither Saint Peter nor any other apostle had coercive jurisdiction over the remaining apostles or other aforementioned ecclesiastical ministers. From this it additionally follows by necessity that the Roman bishop as well as all aforementioned ecclesiastical ministers are subject in property and person to the coercive jurisdiction of the judges and government under the authority of the human legislator; and one can and ought to grasp this with certainty from the preceding chapter and from *Defensor pacis*, Discourse I, chapters 15 and 17, and Discourse II, chapters 4, 5, 8 and 9.

Chapter 2

[1] Yet someone might object to the preceding by declaring that bishops or priests, or their single assembly, can establish coercive laws and for this reason restrain transgressors just like judges in the present world. For this seems to belong to the power and office of priests and also the single assembly of them, since it is useful and expedient for good morals and for the pursuit of happiness and the avoidance of misery in the future world, because such matters seem to be spiritual in nature.

[2] This allegedly occurs because the statutes of priests are coercive in the present world. For as a result of this, men are led towards good morals and turned away from bad morals, by means of which eternal happiness is achieved and damnation is avoided.

[3] Yet we say that by means of divine law and human coercion, these concerns are in fact sufficiently addressed and resolved for the state of the present as well as the future world. For this reason, anything established by priests or their single assembly is totally useless. This is both because the minor premise of the aforementioned syllogism is to be rejected pure and simple and because it is inexpedient and useless by reason of the inconvenience which follows from it.

[4] First, such law results from an inadequate legislator, since it is neither human nor divine; that it is not human is demonstrated in *Defensor pacis*, Discourse I, chapters 12 and 13; that it is not divine is demonstrated by James 4[:12] and I Peter 2 [II Peter 1:21] and by what is known to all those faithful to Christ.

[5] There also follows from this another inconvenience, since there come to be several coercive human legislators and governments ruling over the same multitude, none of which occupies a subordinate position in the present world, creating a situation which is particularly unbearable for the polity [*politia*]. Up until the present this has been a cause of perpetual dissension among those faithful to Christ, except when power or authority was snatched entirely away by the usurpation of one of the aforementioned clerics. This is also impossible and unbearable for the polity and citizens because of the inconveniences which follow from it, which are clearly demonstrated in *Defensor pacis*, Discourse I, chapter 17.

There is also a third inconvenience that follows from the preceding. Let us suppose that priests have an equal right [*ratio*] to establish coercive law, and to exercise judgement according to such law over all civil human acts in the present world, because all such acts, which human law enjoins or prohibits, touch upon good or bad morals. For this reason, the law is described by the human legislator in this way: the law is a holy sanction, enjoining just and honourable conduct and prohibiting dishonourable acts. It would also follow, therefore, that priests would be the human legislators and that the laws of the citizens would be superfluous. The opposite of this is demonstrated in *Defensor pacis*, Discourse I, chapters 11, 12 and 13, and is confirmed by Holy Scripture cited in Discourse II, chapters 4, 5, 8 and 9.

[6] But some people say that although this power does not pertain regularly and without reservation to the office of the priest, still in special cases (*in casu*) it pertains to their office, for instance, should rulers on account of some defect be negligent regarding matters of legislation or in the discharge of their lesser obligations. These rhetorical statements are contrary to Scripture and human reason. For the Apostle says in II Timothy 2[:4]: 'No soldier of God involves himself in secular affairs', namely, in litigation or civil matters; and in I Corinthians 6[:4]: 'When therefore you have been permitted judgement in secular cases, those who were appointed to be judges were despised by the church'; and by 'judgement' he means over secular matters or contentions which arise from human action and additionally those uncertainties which arise

5

concerning divine law. For this reason, the same Apostle says in I Corinthians 3[:3]: 'Since jealousy and contention reign among you, are you not carnal', that is, litigating over secular matters, 'and travelling according to the ways of men?' And once more, in II Corinthians 1[:24], he says, 'We will not be lord over your faith'; he is speaking expressly about spiritual matters, as is likewise confirmed by the authority or exposition of Ambrose and Chrysostom regarding these texts, which may be found by whomever cares to check in *Defensor pacis*, Discourse II, chapters 4, 5 and 7.

[7] This position is also contrary to human reason. For the power and authority to correct rulers who are negligent or irresponsible in performing their duties by restraining them through punishment of their persons or property belongs solely to the human legislator, as is demonstrated in *Defensor pacis*, Discourse I, chapters 15 and 18. And I say furthermore that if such correction pertains to some particular part or office of the civic body, then under no circumstances does it pertain to the priests, but instead to the men of prudence [*prudentes*] or learned teachers, indeed preferably to the workmen or craftsmen or the rest of the labourers [*mechanicis*]. For it is not forbidden by human reason or law, or by Holy Scripture, by counsel or by precept, for these men to involve themselves in civil or secular activities. This is forbidden to priests and bishops, however, as we have already indicated on the authority of the Apostle. And I say that while, according to the Apostle, it can pertain to the office of the priest to engage in 'exhortation, submission, censure and reproof, with patience and instruction in all things' [II Timothy 4:2], he can never engage in compulsion. For this reason, Ambrose in 'On Surrendering the Basilica' says this to the Emperor Constantine: 'I shall suffer, I shall mourn, I shall cry; against armies, even the Goths, my weapons are my tears; for such are the defences of priests; for they neither can nor ought otherwise to resist.'[1]

Chapter 3

[1] As to the question of whether, if the whole multitude of the faithful or its greater part or rulers wished to stray from the faith of Christ, or did in fact stray, they should or could be restrained to the contrary by the priests or their assembly, it must always be answered in the negative, as is apparent from the admonition of Christ in Matthew 10[:23], in so far as

He says, 'If they have persecuted you in one city, take refuge in another'. For this reason, He willed for the apostles and their successors, the bishops or presbyters, to abstain not only from compelling others but even from the defence of their own bodies, which the Apostle also decreed in the already cited passage: 'We are not lord over your faith'. Yet certain people insist that something else was meant by the Apostle, in so far as he says in II Corinthians 1[:23]: 'It was to spare you that I did not come to Corinth'; and once again in I Corinthians 4[:21]: 'Is it for you to determine? Do I come to you with a cane or in gentleness?' This is stated more fully in II Corinthians 10[:6]: 'We are ready to avenge all disobedience once your obedience is complete'.

[2] Yet to this and similar observations it may be responded that such correction is verbal, not coercive, namely, the censuring and reproving of offenders. For this reason, the Apostle said in a passage cited above: 'It was to spare you', etc., adding, 'We will not be lord over your faith'. About this Ambrose remarked: 'And lest he put to shame the Corinthians, as though out of lordship, the Apostle added, "We will not be lord over your faith", that is, your faith does not suffer under lordship or coercion, since it is voluntary, not necessary; for the condition of faith is formed by means of love, not lordship'.[2] These passages are also presented fully in *Defensor pacis*, Discourse II, chapters 5 and 9. In addition, the Apostle said in the passage from [II] Corinthians [10:4] cited above: 'The weapons of our soldiers are not carnal' but are spiritual or verbal. By contrast, those weapons by which men are constrained are carnal, that is, material or corporeal.

[3] Whether the restraint of heretics in this world by punishment of their persons or property and their exclusion from the company of others is a precept or only a counsel according to Holy Scripture, and also who has the authority to do so, are discussed adequately in *Defensor pacis*, Discourse II, chapter 10.

[4] And since neither priests nor their single assembly have such authority and right, we will move on from this topic to a third conclusion that may be asserted about interdiction and excommunication, and which follows by necessity from earlier premises. It is that, by virtue of the words of the Holy Scripture of the New Testament, no bishop or priest or whatever ecclesiastical minister one cares to name, whether communally or separately, can claim for himself any movable or immovable property which has been conceded to him in whole or in part and for which he is obliged to the faithful (excepting adequate food and clothing

alone), especially in as much as such things are claimed by right of lordship [*dominium*]. For as Christ says in John 20[:21]: 'Just as the Father sent me, so I send you also', namely, for the sake of humility and the exercise of priestly office, a view which is also understood to apply to His successors in so far as He says in the twenty-eighth and final chapter of Matthew [28:20]: 'I am with you to the end of the world', which cannot be true of the first apostles unless by it is understood their successors also. Neither Christ nor any of His apostles had allocated to themselves any fixed portion of the goods of the temporal world, especially as regards lordship, but they had only elicited for themselves food and clothing from among the temporal goods offered to them by the faithful. For this reason, Christ says in Matthew 10[:10]: 'The workman is deserving of his sustenance'; and the Apostle remarks in I Timothy 6[:8]: 'As long as we are fed and clothed, let us be content with this', just as the Apostle also says similar things in I Corinthians 9[:9–10] and Romans 15[:27] which are quoted above and have been omitted for the sake of brevity.

[5] Christ rejected all the rest of those temporal possessions that were clearly superfluous, whether held personally or communally, and His apostles were counselled and taught similar rejection, in so far as He says in Matthew 8[:20] and Luke 9[:58]: 'Foxes have holes and the birds of the air have nests, but the son of Man does not have a place where He lays His head'. And moreover, in Luke 14[:33] He speaks to the apostles and through their persons admonishes their successors: 'So therefore none among you can be my disciples who does not renounce everything which you possess'. And since what is not possible is equivalent to what is impossible, some learned holy theologians aim to teach that Christ forbade lordship over temporal goods to His apostles and their successors not only as a matter of counsel but as a precept. We have discussed carefully all such matters and many other issues concerning the poverty of Christ in *Defensor pacis*, Discourse II, chapters 12, 13 and 14. From this it also follows by necessity that neither the apostles of Christ nor their successors – whether priests or bishops or the remaining ministers of the temple – can allocate or claim a tenth or other fixed portion of movable or immovable temporal goods. For this reason, according to II Corinthians 9[:7], the Apostle requested alms or contributions for those Christian believers living in Jerusalem, because they had sold their farms and houses and had laid the proceeds at the feet of the apostles for distribution to the community of the faithful, as is written in Acts 4[:34–5], where it states: 'Everyone gave according to what his heart had

resolved, none out of necessity', that is, not by coercion. For this reason, the Apostle also adds [in II Corinthians 8:8, 10]: 'I do not speak like a commander . . . but I give counsel in this matter'. And if the Corinthians had nevertheless owed such tithes by obligation to the divine law, the Apostle would not have said: 'I do not speak like a commander', nor would it be said: 'Everyone gave according to what his heart had resolved', but the tithe would have been exacted from them just as though the divine law required this.

[6] Moreover, if Christ had reserved for Himself and His apostles such tithes and lordship to be owed by the faithful, He would have provided not only for the immediate future but also for times in the more distant future, and consequently He would not have been poor nor would He have experienced great poverty along with the apostles. Yet the opposite is made clearly apparent by Holy Scripture, as is carefully presented in *Defensor pacis*, Discourse II, chapters 12, 13 and 14.

[7] From this, one can also infer that because certain laymen as well as certain clerics had obtained such tithes from the earliest times of antiquity by means of the documents or privileges of the Roman ruler, and had possessed such tithes in good faith without any civil or ecclesiastical censure as regards tribute and taxes and concessions and very many other arrangements pertaining to the authority of the Roman ruler, therefore these were transferred and conceded to them by the supreme human legislator.

[8] Nor may one object that the Old Law mentions tenths and first fruits, since the observance of Mosaic legal and ceremonial practices is not obligatory for those faithful to Christ, because as the Apostle Paul says [Romans 7:6]: 'Freed from the Old Law, we serve law in a new way', and that [Hebrews 7:12] 'with a changed priesthood, it is also necessary that a change be made in the law'. Moreover, such tithes are not, according to the Old Law, owed to the priests but also to all laymen and secular persons who have been assigned to the Tribe of Levi.

Chapter 4

[1] The fourth principal conclusion is that the pronouncement of divine right or law in the second sense pertains to bishops or priests. We read of this sense in Scripture, when in John 20[:21] Christ conceded it to His apostles, saying: 'Just as the Father sent me, so I send you also', and

in the twenty-eighth and final chapter of Matthew [28:19, 20]: 'Go, therefore, teach all nations, baptising them in the name of the Father', etc., 'teaching them to perform all your directives'. Along with the aforementioned power to pronounce or to teach divine right or law, it may be read that Christ had conferred on these same apostles certain other authority to do or perform certain acts on their own, such as baptising, which is already mentioned in the chapter from Matthew, and performing the Eucharist or creation of His body out of bread, in so far as He says in Matthew 26[:26] and Luke 22[:19]: 'For this is my body which is given up for you; do this in memory of me'.

[2] Another of these powers is the appointment of successors in priestly office and of other ministers who are called deacons. Regarding this the Apostle speaks in I Timothy 4[:14]: 'Do not neglect that gift which is within you, which was given to you by the prophets and by the laying of hands by the presbyters'; and in Titus 1[:5]: 'I left you behind in Crete in order that arrangements might be undertaken and presbyters be constituted for each city', etc.; and once again, in Acts 4 [6:6] it says: 'These', namely, deacons, 'were at the feet of the apostles, and they laid their hands upon them while praying'. And yet again, it may be read that Christ had conceded certain other forms of authority to the apostles of whom we now speak such as that of binding and loosing human beings from sin the present world, in order that happiness and also misery are achieved or avoided in the future world. And perhaps Christ conceded to them other forms of authority, according to divine law, about which there is no pressing need to debate for the present.

[3] None of the preceding powers or forms of authority is coercive; but all are instructional or managerial [*oeconomica*], whether speculative or practical, just like those which a physician exercises in counselling and treating healthy and ill persons. One may discover the clear similarity of this comparison in *Defensor pacis*, Discourse II, chapters 6, 7 and 9, and more certainly yet in chapters 4 and 5 of the same Discourse. And consequently, when power is called spiritual, such power should not be understood as jurisdiction or authority in the sense of the coercive punishment of persons or their property in the present world, but as that kind of instruction or practice, exhortation and censure which we already ascribed to the power of the physician or steward [*oeconomi*]. Yet disregarding all the powers mentioned, it is necessary to discuss at present the single greatest power, which is the binding and loosing of human beings from sin, and which is commonly called 'the power of the

keys' by holy men and learned teachers of the Holy Scripture. A great
deal has been said about this power, and to what extent it may be
conceded to bishops or priests, in *Defensor pacis*, Discourse II, chapters 6
and 7, in accordance with the words of the Master of the 'Sentences' and
other holy and learned men whose names are included in the same
chapters. And as it may be compressed by way of summary, the Master
concludes that this power of priests to loose and bind, remit or uphold,
sin is nothing other than declaring, in full view of the church, which sins
are to be remitted or upheld, diminished or released, by God for one's
condition in the future world, towards the end of the punishment of
transgressors and the pursuit of happiness. For this reason, he says:
'Priests, who are the physicians of the soul, neither uphold nor remit sins,
but only give a prognosis. For it is God alone who by Himself upholds or
remits their sins'.[3] And the Master adds that there is another way of
binding and loosing sinners by priests in the present world, namely, the
infliction of punishment on sinners or the imposition of penitence upon
someone for sins in the present world, for the sake of avoiding
punishment wholly or in part in the future world. For this reason, the
Master, whose authority is Pope Leo, also says that 'priests perform
works of justice upon sinners in so far as they bind them with the debt of
penitence or punishment; yet in so far as they halt or relax the
punishment, they perform works of mercy'.[4]

Chapter 5

[1] On the basis of this authority of priests, which is commonly called
the power of the keys, some people infer several conclusions. And the first
of these is that it is necessary for eternal deliverance that every human
being confess to a priest all sins, hidden as well as manifest, committed
against the precepts of divine law, which are commonly called mortal sins
or those liable to yield eternal damnation.

[2] From this some people infer another conclusion, namely, that on
the basis of the aforementioned authority priests can inflict upon the
persons or property of sinners punishment or penance in the present
world, in order that their sins might be removed by these means; and also
that on account of the sinner's need for deliverance, he may not be
otherwise absolved from sin.

[3] By reason of the extension of this power, in addition, they infer

another conclusion: that presbyters or bishops, especially the Roman bishop, can confer indulgence of punishment in the future world for a certain length of time in years, months and days and even for all times, as is proclaimed at the end of each century, upon those offering them presents or other temporal gifts, or upon pilgrims who out of reverence travel from place to place visiting basilicas and houses of the holy, and similarly upon those who travel across the ocean in order to subdue or otherwise constrain the infidels.

[4] And once again, others infer from the above mentioned authority of the keys, and the plenitude of power owed especially to the bishop of Rome, the conclusion that the same bishop, and the rest of the bishops and priests to whom the Roman bishop wishes to concede or entrust it, can absolve any one of the faithful from a vow or the uttering of a vow, so that he is not at all bound to the observation of the vow.

[5] From the above, others infer on the basis of the aforementioned authority the conclusion that individual bishops or presbyters or the single assembly of bishops can excommunicate each one of the faithful for committing sin, such that they can deprive each one of these excommunicates and the communicates themselves of the decision of whom shall, by offering prayer in church, be present before God. They say that priests can deprive the disobedient sinner not only of this but also of other things and, in so far as their word prevails, they in fact deprive him of all civil association, since they deny the company of the faithful themselves to those not obediently performing the divine offices. They call the deprivation or denial of these and other sacraments of the church 'ecclesiastical interdicts'. In all these and in the remaining spiritual powers, they say that the Roman bishop above all others, by reason of succession to Saint Peter, has a plenitude of power. Modern Roman bishops along with their clerics who are called cardinals have proclaimed that what is owed to them on the basis of this plenitude of power extends to lordship over all principalities and as a consequence over all civil acts and also over all temporal goods.

[6] It is therefore the first conclusion which some people infer from the power of the keys previously claimed for and owed to priests that anyone faithful to Christ is bound out of the necessity of eternal salvation to confess to a priest the commission of mortal sins by himself. They ascribe this to what is said by the Holy Scripture in the last chapter of James [5:16], which states: 'Confess your sins to one another'. Moreover, they assert this on the authority of Augustine and certain other holy men and

learned teachers, whose words the Master of the 'Sentences' presents in Book 4, Distinction 17, Chapter 4. This set of quotations is omitted for reason of brevity and because those who might care can look at the same text.

[7] They also endeavour to demonstrate the same conclusion by an argument derived from absurdity or impossibility according to Scripture, for if the confession of such sins should not be necessary, then the authority or power of the sacerdotal keys would have been handed without reason to the apostles and their successors; this view is to be shunned as heretical.

[8] We say, however, that according to the Holy Scripture, one can never prove that such confession of sins is to be made out of necessity of eternal salvation, but only out of utility and perhaps expedience, as a counsel rather than a precept of Holy Scripture. Rather, it is sufficient to confess one's sins to God alone, namely, to acknowledge them and to pay a penalty for them with the intent of not committing such sins again in the future. For one reads that the Psalmist has declared and also done this: 'I confess to you, Lord, with all my heart' [Psalm 9:1]; and once again, Psalms [106:1] says: 'Confess to the Lord, since it is good', etc. Moreover, one reads that Christ has said and done the same, in so far as Matthew 11[:25] says: 'I confess to you, Lord, Father of the heavens and the earth', while the curious may find for themselves many other, similar statements in the Scriptures.

Nor may it be objected further that they have introduced contrary evidence from James. For James does not say: 'Confess to priests' but 'Confess your sins to one another', indicating the Christian faithful without distinction and these were words of counsel rather than precept. For this reason, a certain gloss says: 'Confess your sins to one another in order to avoid pride'.

[9] Regarding the authority of Augustine and also the other holy men and learned teachers whose views the Master of the 'Sentences' had presented above, it may be said that the saints and learned men believed such confessions of sin to be counsels rather than precepts of Holy Scripture. And what we have said is expressly affirmed by Chrysostom, whose authority and importance is adduced by the Master of the same work; and the reciting of this has been omitted for reason of brevity.

[10] And as a result, even if Augustine along with the aforementioned saints and learned teachers had believed the confession of sins mentioned before to be a precept of divine law, and that no one can be saved eternally

without it, still I reject their beliefs, since they are not based on Holy Scripture or canon nor are they deduced from the canons or Holy Scripture, and since Chrysostom has expressly written the opposite, as is stated above.

[11] Regarding the argument which was derived from impossibility, namely, that the sacerdotal keys or authority to loose and also to bind, would be groundless if believers in Christ were not obligated out of necessity of eternal salvation to make such a confession of sins to priests, the consequent is to be rejected. For should there never have been such a confession of sins, still the authority of the keys or power of binding and loosing is certainly very useful for eternal salvation and for recalling human beings from sins they are committing or have committed, hidden as well as manifest.

[12] For priests proclaim and denounce in full view of the church the sins which men are committing or plan to commit, and either they do not repent of them, but, persisting in doing or planning such acts, they are made liable to eternal damnation, or, repenting or regaining their senses about what they have done or plan to do, the sinners repent of the commission of sin and are absolved from the already mentioned eternal damnation. They examine themselves and grieve before God, and they are deterred from planning to commit other such acts by the fear of future punishment that has been aroused in them by priests.

[13] And this is the office and authority of the priesthood which we have previously called the power of the keys or of binding and loosing. And this method of loosing and binding sinners can certainly be useful without the above mentioned confession. This may also be demonstrated through an argument deduced by necessity from Holy Scripture: since confession, or the intention by someone to confess sins to a priest, is not necessary for someone to be bound in the present world to guilt and the punishment of eternal damnation, therefore confession is not necessary, etc., in order for someone to be absolved from guilt and punishment. The antecedent is widely known on the basis of Scripture, since each sinner is bound by the commission of wrongdoing to the guilt and punishment mentioned above without any priests whomsoever knowing it. For this reason, Scripture says: 'If your eye should cause you to sin, tear it out', etc., 'because it is better to have one eye', etc., 'than to have two eyes in the flames of punishment' [Matthew 18:9]. And once again, the Apostle states in Timothy [Titus 3:10–11]: 'The heretical man', etc., 'is to be shunned; for he is condemned by his own judgement', that is, made

guilty, and this is a necessary consequence of many other passages in the Holy Scriptures, since one and the same authority of priests to bind and loose human beings from sin exists throughout. Therefore, since their action in the binding of sinners is not necessitated by this authority, etc., hence it is similarly unnecessary in the loosing of them, but simple contrition and true repentance of the commission suffices without ever making or having made a confession to a priest, in so far as one may be absolved immediately by God. For this reason, the Psalmist says: 'God does not will the death of a sinner, but he will be transformed and gain life' [Ezekiel 33:11]. And once again: 'Do not scorn, God, a contrite and humble heart' [Psalm 51:17]. Priests do not, therefore, loose or bind from sin other than as was described earlier. Nothing else I said above or will say below is claimed obstinately. It is instead argued and responded to logically, and also may be read in the judgements of others, that if a confession is made by a sinner of any of his sins to a priest, and he does not desist from committing the sin as a result of the priest's admonition, and moreover does not produce one or two witnesses in his defence as a result of the priest's admonition, then the priest is bound and must reveal the commission of such sins in full view of the whole church. If the sinner does not heed the correction or reproach of the church, then he ought to be bound or be proclaimed to be bound by the punishment of eternal damnation as a result of the authority of priests to loose and also to bind, that is, the power of the keys. If he truly repents of sin and regains his senses, he should be proclaimed to be absolved of the previously stated punishment by the power of priests. This point also seems to resound clearly in the scriptural words of Matthew 18[:15–18], which are spoken to all faithful Christians without distinction, priests as well as non-priests, according to this passage: 'If your brother has sinned before you, rebuke him between yourselves; if he heeds you, you have won back your brother; if he does not heed you, bring one or two witnesses along with you, since every dispute rests upon the words of two or three people; if he does not heed these, tell the church; if he does not heed the church, he is to you like a heathen or a tax collector.' And it is then appended that Christ said in spiritual fashion to his apostles: 'I tell you truly that whatever you have bound on earth will be bound in heaven; and whatever you have loosed on earth will be loosed in heaven'. Thus, Christ said: 'If your brother has sinned before you', etc. Some have not explicated this passage in accordance with the intention of the Scripture, as it appears there, saying instead: 'If your brother has sinned towards you, that is, against you; for either your brother has sinned against you or against those close to you; if it is known to you, you ought to rebuke him, since in either instance, the reason for the correction is the same, namely, in order to win your brother'. But one might gloss this passage differently, namely, 'If your brother has sinned before you', that is, if it is known to you alone, whether against those close to you or against you yourself. And this exposition is consonant with Scripture and is proven by the very Scripture itself, since in what comes next the reason for the correction continues to be the same, as we have said above, in so far as after that it then follows: 'Bring one or two witnesses along with you, since every dispute rests upon the words of two or three people'. For if the Scripture is understood as meaning that a brother is to be rebuked for a sinful act against you alone, then even if two witnesses have been brought along with you, the dispute would not rest before the multitude upon the words of three witnesses. For in a trial before the church, the plaintiff [*accusator*] is not accepted as a witness, since he may be suspected of malevolence. And therefore, if there ought to be testimony from three persons against a sinner in full view of the multitude, it must be from you and two others whom you have brought along with you, and must not be about a sin committed against you but rather against a brother. Therefore, the Scripture says: 'If your brother has sinned before you, rebuke him between yourselves', and do not defame him; 'if he does not heed you, bring witnesses', so that he may be ashamed; 'if he does not heed these, tell the church', so that he may be defamed and recalled. It may be added to the gloss that one is not capable of pride who has been humbled by such correction from the multitude, that is, by public disgrace. Christ adds: 'Whatever you have bound', etc., bestowing upon the apostles the power to proclaim that such sinners are sentenced or have been sentenced by God to perpetual damnation in the future world, so that on account of their terror and fear sinners may be recalled from sins committed or yet to be committed.

Therefore, should these words – 'If your brother has sinned before you', etc. – on the one hand, have been spoken by Christ to priests alone, in such case they can and should follow the counsel or precept of Christ by disclosing sin in full view of the church, according to the method we have described. On the other hand, if He said this to all without distinction, priests as well as non-priests, then the same thing follows from the premises, namely, that priests are permitted to disclose sins whenever they are confessed to them in accordance with the method already mentioned in the preceding, which is what the Apostle also believed, in as much as he says in [I] Timothy [5:20]: 'Censure sinners before all, in order that others will be fearful'.

[14] But someone might say: if there is no other priestly power of binding and also of loosing except that of divulgence in full view of the church, since the bound and the loosed are bound and loosed before God, then it would seem that those who are not priests, especially those having knowledge of Holy Scripture, can bind or loose transgressors, since they are capable of and know about the proclamation of such matters. Moreover, the words of Christ mentioned above may be understood in terms of such a method of loosing and binding, as Augustine seems to believe, since he states it in a certain homily.[5]

[15] We say, however, that a priest binds and looses men on account of sin in a different way than does a brother to brothers by way of making them liable for the performance of an injury. For we see in secular courts that, when someone inflicts an injury upon another, he is made liable to a double punishment: namely, one for the injured or offended party and another for the community or judge. Indeed, the injured or offended party can, if it would wish, forgive the debt owed by the offending party to the injured party, or it can exact the punishment from the same party. But the punishment owed by the offending or injuring party to the community or judge can by no means be remitted by the injured party. This similarly extends also to the spiritual judgements imposed by God in the future world. For on account of injuries committed amongst brothers against divine law, the sinner or criminal is similarly made liable to two punishments in his otherworldly condition: one is the offense against the brother, namely, that which can be remitted to the offending party. This matter is spoken and prayed about in the Lord's Prayer: 'Forgive us our debts as we forgive those who are indebted to us' [Matthew 6:12]. The sinner is also made liable to another punishment by way of his injury against God, and the offended party is not able to remit the offending party, but God alone can do this.

[16] Thus, priests loose and bind differently according to the authority or power they were given by Christ along with a disposition [*habitus*] or character, which is itself a disposition, and which is commonly called the sacerdotal form or character of 'the gift given by the prophet', according to the Apostle in [I] Timothy [4:14]. For this reason, although someone skilled in the Holy Scripture may know the means by which a sinner is bound by and loosed from sin, as well as the pains and punishment of

eternal damnation which accompany loosing and binding in the future world, not to mention full knowledge of how these are proclaimed in church, still he neither can nor should perform these functions unless this sacerdotal authority is first conceded to him by God and those to whom the ministry of God pertains. Consequently, when it has been said that non-priests learned in the Holy Scripture would seem capable of loosing and binding sinners in full view of the church, this is to be entirely rejected, since although they know, still they do not have the exercise of this power from Christ, who grants such authority. For this reason, the Apostle in Romans 10[:15] asks in regard to this subject: 'How will they have a preacher unless one is sent?' since no one should fail to cease teaching about spiritual matters or administering the sacrament 'unless he is sent', that is, by having authority from those who have the power to confer such authority.

[17] From this, it is clearly apparent that what was said immediately before poses no obstacle. This is seen adequately from the physician of the body, whose art may be set analogously alongside that of the priest, just as Christ called Himself by the name of physician in Luke 5[:31]: 'Those who are healthy are not in need of a physician'. For someone may have the disposition [*habitus*] by means of which he can explain and judge health and illness, and similarly can provide care for them. Yet if he is lacking the licence or authority to teach or provide care, which is to be entrusted to him by the human legislator or ruler, then he is not permitted to teach medicine nor to provide medical care for healthy and ill people. Instead, the practice of medicine transgresses human law in a punishable manner if someone has been prohibited by such authority from providing that care.

[18] Regarding the authority of Augustine invoked above, it may be said that by this he explained the type of loosing and binding by means of which brothers can bind and loose brothers from injuries performed by one to the other. Yet in the homily mentioned before he does not expound on the same words of Christ or Scripture invoked above, namely, 'I tell you truly that whatever you have bound', etc. For these words of Scripture should be understood according to the preceding gloss on the power of binding and loosing that Christ bestowed on the apostles.

[19] Once again, someone might insist that each one of the Christian faithful is bound to confess sins to the priesthood out of necessity of eternal salvation, and that the sinner refusing to do this is condemned eternally. For that which is made a precept or statute by a general council

or the universal Church is bound to be observed by each one of the Christian faithful under pain of eternal damnation. The confessing of sins to priests has been made a precept or statute for every one of the Christian faithful. Thus, each one of the Christian faithful is obligated to make such confession to a priest.

[20] We say, however, that precepts or statutes of the universal Church or general council which are not enjoined or prohibited by Holy Scripture but which only relate to ecclesiastical ritual, and those remaining matters which fall under the heading of counsel rather than precept, touch every one of the Christian faithful in general, clerics as well as laymen. The precepts of a general council endure for all those faithful Christians, clerics as well as laymen, who have extended their consent in this council, whether by their own act or through their syndics, to such statutes or precepts, in so far as there must be observance of these statutes by every one of the faithful out of necessity of eternal salvation, at least so long as they have not been revoked by the above mentioned council or are not related to the immediate precepts of divine law, since no divine law can be revoked by human beings or the human community. But the Christian faithful are obligated to such precepts and human statutes so long as they have not been revoked by the general council because human laws and decrees are useful for the common utility of human beings either without reservation or for the moment. No faithful Christian is permitted to act against or depart from them without sinning mortally, because we say that there must be observance of them out of necessity of eternal salvation.

[21] Something is said in the sixth conclusion of the second section [chapter 10] about the matter of how confessions should be made to priests by those faithful to Christ if such confessions were a precept or statute or had been ordained by a general council of all faithful Christians by the above method, so long as such precepts or statute had not been revoked by the decree of the same council.

Chapter 6

[1] The second conclusion which some people infer from the power of the keys under discussion is that any priest can inflict punishment upon persons or their property or penance upon sinners in this world, to which sinners submit and which they undergo in proportion to their ability,

and that a sinner may not be otherwise loosed from sin. This opinion is recited by the Master of the 'Sentences' in Book IV, Distinction 18, Chapter 6, and the same text seems to agree on the method according to which priests loose sinners: it is done in full view of the church, they bind those deserving of punishment, and they impose a suitable penance on them.

With due reverence to the Master and others asserting this view, however, we say that one cannot demonstrate by means of the Holy Scripture that this power or authority pertains to priests, nor can one demonstrate that something else follows by necessity from it, such as the quantity and quality of the punishments that are owing to the sinner in the future world for sins committed by him in this world. Even if someone perhaps has a divine revelation about this, we are nevertheless not bound out of the necessity of eternal salvation to believe or obey any of what has been said by him about such a revelation, unless we wish to do so. As a result, one can reject on grounds of probability the opinion which the Master and also others have asserted, since their words are not entailed by logical necessity from their first premise. From this, it is also evident that the sinner who has confessed and truly repented of sin is to be absolved from the punishment of eternal damnation, even though he has never rendered penance in his person or his property for his sin in the present world. For this reason, it is a counsel, but not a precept, to perform penance for sin in the present world.

Chapter 7

[1] There is once more a certain other conclusion mentioned above which some people infer from the power of the keys already discussed: that priests and bishops, and especially the Roman bishop, can concede to sinners indulgence for punishment in the future world for sins committed by them in the present world, for a fixed period of time, such as years, months and days, and occasionally for the whole of time, as happens to those who travel to Rome at the end of each century. Just as one cannot demonstrate their possession of this authority according to Holy Scripture nor can it be deduced by necessity from Scripture, so for the same reasons and by the same arguments as those stated immediately above about the power of imposing penance in the present world for sin, we must reject the power put forward on their behalf, namely, the preceding

conferment of indulgence. Although we concede that, through their prayers for sinners, punishment for sins may be reduced, in quantity or quality and in proportion to penance for sin, by God in the other world, this is only invoked by a priest (if he invokes it at all) as counsel and not as precept. But no one is bound out of necessity of eternal salvation to believe in either the size or the nature of this power in the way priests have claimed and assigned it in their sermons and writings.

[2] From this and on account of the same reasons, one can and should also infer that neither priests alone, either separately or communally, nor the Roman bishop have the authority or power to order or command any of the faithful to perform any fast regardless of length or to forbid food to anyone, nor to command likewise a holiday from manual or civil labours on certain days on account of the festivals of saints, nor conversely to forbid such decrees under threat of the infliction of punishment in the condition of either the present or future world. But this falls to the authority of the human legislator or the general council of all faithful Christians or of those who stand in place [*vicem repraesentant*] of all faithful Christians. Whether those who go on foreign journeys and pilgrimages to visit the shrines of saints are meritorious, and whether they may accordingly receive whole or partial indulgence in the other world for their sins, remains to be discussed.

[3] And I say, in accordance with what we have set forth already, that one cannot prove on the basis of Holy Scripture that any individual ought to be compelled to confess to a faithful Christian, just as is also declared and made evident through the same Scripture and the statements of the saints in *Defensor pacis*, Discourse II, chapters 4, 5 and 9. From this, it follows that if a foreign journey is made or will be made in order to subdue or restrain infidels for the sake of the Christian faith, then such a foreign journey would in no way seem to be meritorious. But if such a foreign journey is to be made in order to obey the Roman ruler and people in civil precepts and in order that the tribute owed to them may be surrendered, as is their right, then I think that such a trip should be considered meritorious for the sake of the peace and tranquillity of all who live civilly.

[4] Regarding pilgrimages which are made by sinners in order to visit the shrines of saints out of reverence, I say that these can be meritorious. But I would nevertheless add that if the same worldly goods or riches which a person spends to do the foregoing would be distributed to the poor (for example, to widows, orphans and the disabled, or the infirm or

other needy persons, or the undefiled, or others who are burdened by large families or needy children, or who are indigent, honourable paupers in any way whatsoever) or on account of the defence of the republic when necessity threatens it, then such an act merits forgiveness before God a hundred times more than the aforementioned visitation of shrines on account of reverence for saints. For we do not find counsels or precepts about the making of such pilgrimages in Scripture, but one may locate clear counsels in the Old Law as well as the New about the preceding alms-giving and distribution of worldly goods or riches to the poor already mentioned. For the Psalmist has said: 'Redeem your sins by alms-giving' [Daniel 4:27] and in Luke 11 and 12 and numerous other places in Scripture, Christ says: 'Go and sell everything you have and give it to the poor' [Luke 12:33]. Moreover, Christ laments about those who are able to do this but do not do it, as He says in Matthew 25[:42–43]: 'I was hungry, and you did not give me something to eat; thirsty, and you did not give me water; I was naked, and you did not clothe me', taking upon Himself all of these in the person of the poor; and nowhere is it written that He had said: 'I was in Rome and Jerusalem and you did not visit me'. Furthermore, although such pilgrimages to more distant places are most often made in order to see strange and foreign provinces and locales rather than on account of the devotion which one ought to have in such matters (and I say, in short, that one is to take note of such things), still those which are made by sinners either as a penance in their persons and property for some sin in the present world or as overseas trips for the purpose stated before, namely, the aiding of the republic, or as pilgrimages with a similar goal, should result in the total or partial forgiveness of their sins in the future world. It is also the case that such indulgence or forgiveness is never conceded to them by bishops or priests, for bishops or priests have no power to grant or refuse such indulgence to sinners, but it belongs only to God, who alone knows the inner condition of sinners and the hearts of penitents as well as the quality and quantity of the penance to be offered by those who are deserving or blameworthy.

Chapter 8

[1] Once again, it is the conclusion of some people, who infer something from the already mentioned authority of the keys and that

plenitude of power which they ascribe to the Roman bishop, namely, that the same Roman bishop (who is called pope), and the other bishops and priests to whom he has willed to entrust or concede this power, can absolve or free anyone faithful to Christ from any vow whatsoever through releasing them from what has been uttered, so that the person is henceforth not at all bound to the observation of the vow mentioned above. In order to consider this inference more clearly, it is necessary to enquire, first, about what a vow is; second, about which people can swear or utter a vow and similarly be obligated to the observance of it; third, about which vows can and ought to be uttered; and finally, about to whom and on what account the preceding vow should be sworn.

[2] Regarding the first item on our list, therefore, we say that a vow, according to what many judge, is a sort of voluntary promise made by the mind or in words to do or refrain from doing something with adequate knowledge or cognisance of it in order to attain some goal in the present or future world. Regarding the second matter, I say that a person swearing a vow should utter it at that age at which one is presumed by legal judgement or conventional practice to possess reason, which prudent men estimate among humans of the male gender to be fifteen years and determine among females to be twelve years.

[3] Now in relation to the third issue, it ought not to escape our notice that in regard to the commission or omission of those human acts in connection with which vows may be uttered, some are classified under the precepts of human or divine law. Certain of these can be classified in terms of the permission of human as well as divine law; others are classified under counsel, which is directed to divine rather than to human law. In regard to the differences between affirmative precepts, by which the laws permit something, and negative precepts, which are customarily called prohibitions, and also between precepts and counsels, enough is said by us in *Defensor pacis*, Discourse II, chapters 8 and 12. Returning to those matters which detain us for present purposes, we say that precepts or prohibitions of divine as well as human law are not classified as vows, and no one may utter a vow in regard to them, since human beings of either gender are obligated under threat of punishment in the present condition or the future world or both to be observant of all divine as well as human laws, precisely because human laws do not contradict divine laws. For divine law commands obedience to human rulers and laws which are not contrary to divine law, just as was previously demonstrated by Christ and the apostles. Regarding certain acts permitted by divine or

human laws, one may likewise not utter a vow, such as the gift of my clothes to clowns, or my not giving them, or the organization of a banquet for other people, or its non-organization, and other quite similar matters the enjoyment of which in the present life may not be denied to those swearing vows by reason of reverence to God or some blessed spirit; one may not utter a vow about such matters, for one is not obligated to observe them under threat of some punishment in the present or future world. Yet vows are customarily uttered regarding most acts permitted by human as well as divine law, and regarding those matters which are properly called counsels in accordance with divine law on account of earning some merit or avoiding evil in the condition of the present or future world; human beings seem obligated to observe these vows, as will become more evident from what is being said. One may take an example of this: if a vow has been uttered about some act to be committed or omitted, such as if one has a son by one's wife, if one defeats one's enemies, if one obtains a profit, if one avoids the perils of land or water, if one recovers one's health, if one avoids imprisonment, and the rest of the same sort of things desired or shunned in the condition and for the condition of this world; likewise, one may utter a vow regarding those matters which are properly named counsels of divine law in order to achieve greater or lesser happiness or to avoid greater or lesser misery for the condition not of the present but of the future world. In the definition of a vow developed in the foregoing, we said that a vow is a voluntary human promise, classified under counsel rather than precept, made by the mind or in words or both by a person of a suitable age about something adequately known or understood which is to be committed or omitted by counsel or permission on account of obtaining or avoiding something by divine grace alone or by the intercession of some blessed spirit in the present or future world. In addition, I say that such a vow can be uttered by those who swear to commit or omit an act either absolutely and without reservation or conditionally, namely, if some other person has agreed to such a vow or in as much as he has agreed to accomplish or refrain from some act.

[4] Having set forth these points, we may consequently infer some conclusions from them: the first of these is that no one is bound or obligated to swear an oath under threat of punishment in the present world, since what is classified solely under counsel or permission, rather than the precept or prohibition of divine or human law, requires no one to receive some punishment in the present or future world. Vows are forms

of permission or counsel rather than the precepts or prohibitions of some law, as should be evident from the previously presented definition of a vow.

Another conclusion is that everyone is obligated to the observance of what is owed by a vow under threat of some punishment. For just as human beings who are permitted by human law to commit or omit some act are obligated to the observance of their legitimate [*ex licita causa*] promises under threat of civil punishment, so likewise what is promised to God obliges the swearer or promiser to the observance of the vow under the threat of some punishment, for instance, in the future world, a view which seems to be in accordance with Holy Scripture. For the Psalmist says: 'I have rendered to the Lord my vow' [Psalm 116:14] and additionally Christ says in Matthew 22[:21]: 'Render to Caesar what is Caesar's, and to God what is God's'. Therefore, since those promises which are called vows are made to God legitimately, as is evident from the definition of a vow, it seems that they are likewise to be rendered to God and the swearers are likewise obligated to Him.

[5] The third conclusion is that should an unreserved vow or promise without other conditions have been made to God or some blessed spirit, such as if one has entered into an agreement with another person or in regard to committing or omitting an act for a definite period of time, the Roman bishop or any other bishop or priest cannot absolve the swearer from the vow promised, namely, so that one is not bound at all to the observance of it. The reason for this is that those who are bound civilly cannot be absolved from their obligations by anyone except either by those to whom one is legitimately obligated or by a judge who is superior to the obligated person and to the persons to whom one is obligated. Now, he who swears a legitimate oath to God is obligated to Him, and he is bound in virtue of the vow to render it to Him; he owes nothing at all to the Roman bishop or other priest. If, as we have said, an unreserved or unconditional vow or promise has been made to God or some blessed spirit, neither the Roman bishop nor any other bishop or priest is a judge or superior over the swearer and God or some blessed spirit to whom one has promised to perform what is vowed. Neither the Roman bishop nor any other priest can, therefore, free someone who swears an oath from the aforementioned vow, namely so that one is not obligated by virtue of the vow to render what is due. Moreover, since one does not discover in divine law, especially in writing or commandments, whether under counsel or precept, that the Roman bishop or other priest has such power, one can conclude from it by necessity that no priests have such

authority. We nevertheless say this: that if the vow is not made absolutely and without reservation but conditionally, namely, a vow subject to the arbitration of one or another priest, then such a vow can be relieved by that priest to whose arbitration the uttered vow has been subjected as a result of swearing it; for such a vow is not a promise made without reservation to God, but rather to the priest.

Chapter 9

[1] The fourth conclusion is that no one swearing an oath can by that vow bind another person to the observance of any vow, unless there has been an explicit mandate or precept to do this by a person who has reached the requisite age, as is apparent from the definition of a vow stated above. For a vow is and should be the voluntary and uncoerced swearing of a promise about the committing or omitting of some act which is known rather than unknown, on account of which no one can by the uttering of a vow bind another person involuntarily or unawares to the observance of some vow. From this it would seem to follow that the uttering of vows by Western priests, whether in accordance with a council or outside of their general council, about not accepting wives or about other such counsels regarding the commission or omission of acts which do not touch upon the precepts of divine law or pertain to the office of priests, such as fasting or other such counsels, do not obligate their successors or those following them in the priestly office to perform or observe such oaths, since these would not be known or willed by the succeeding priests. For this reason, they are in no way bound to the observance of a vow under threat of earthly or future punishment, except perhaps should this have been established afterwards by the human legislator, in so far as no one may assume the office of priest unless he has willed his explicit intention to be bound by such counsels or vows. For the identical reason and on the same basis, I also say that none of the religious, whether monks or mendicants or members of other professions regardless of the name by which they are called, can be obligated or bound to observe some new vow or promise made by their society (*collegium*) beyond the profession uttered by them and related to the aforementioned rule, unless such new statute or vow is included by their society in the profession of the rule to be uttered and follows necessarily from such a profession.

[2] As to whether it is permitted for the swearer of an oath to repudiate an uttered vow, so that he is not obligated thereafter to the observance of the vow under threat of punishment to be inflicted in the future world, it seems safe to say that if this occurs on account of doing something better and pleasing God more, or avoiding something worse (in the sense that it could actually affront God more often and offend Him more greatly), then one can repudiate such a vow, since one should take into consideration whether, by the swearing of an oath, one does what is better and avoids what is worse or whether repudiation is consonant with divine law, and whether such a performance of something better or avoidance of something worse cannot be carried out while holding fast to the vow. And one may adduce proof from this example: should someone swear to God Himself to observe a solitary life in the forest, and then the same person who has sworn this oath is elected to exercise some spiritual rulership, whether an episcopacy or another elevated spiritual rank within the church. And once again, if some man or woman has in his or her adolescence sworn out of reverence to be perpetually chaste or to abstain totally from the temptations of the flesh, and afterwards he or she is plagued by such temptations, so that one might more readily sink into the sin of fornication, it would seem safe to say that the person swearing this oath could repudiate the vow. For the above mentioned and like conditions seem to be included in the vow in order to effect it. Those repudiating a vow on the grounds of good conscience should do so, as we have said, on account of doing what is better or avoiding what is worse, which could not be carried out by them by holding fast to the vow. In the same way, moreover, those repudiating a vow in order to do what is better or avoid what is worse do not render their vow or promise to God any the less, but they are judged to render it all the more. An indication that someone can repudiate an uttered vow on account of the aforementioned or like reasonable grounds is that the Roman bishop and the rest of the priests to whom authority has been given by him claim to, and very often do in fact, absolve those of either sex from an oath uttered outside of the profession of some rule or order, mendicant as well as monastic. The priests say that those repudiating a vow in this way by their licence or consent are no longer obligated to the observance of the vow they swore under threat of punishment in the present or future world. It must also be the case that these vows are uttered by the swearers unreservedly without certain conditions, so that priests have been made capable of recalling swearers from their vows legitimately without sin, as we have

already said that they believe, with the addition that the reason for this legitimacy is not on account of the authority of priests or any bishops, whosoever they are, even the Roman bishop who is called pope; but it is on account of a benign interpretation of the reasons for repudiating a vow, on par with consideration of the judgement and conscience of those who swear oaths, as to whether a bishop or priest may will it or not.

[3] It now remains to examine whether the observance of an uttered vow binds those who have sworn and those who repudiate a vow, even without a pressing reason, to eternal punishment or to a punishment which is not eternal (or for a finite time in the otherworldly condition).

It may be recalled that some vows are made in order to achieve some result for the sake of one's otherworldly condition, the swearing of which never produces an effect at all in the present world. And since such vows are not precepts, but voluntary acts or counsels, and are not made about divine laws but solely about matters of counsel, we say that repudiating those things which are voluntary or at one's pleasure does not bind the swearers to eternal punishment in the future world. But perhaps on account of the fickleness or contempt and bad examples displayed to others by those who do such things, some temporal punishment should be imposed upon those who repudiate oaths. Once again, certain vows are uttered by swearers in order to obtain or avoid or evade something for the sake of one's condition in the present world. If one does not obtain or evade it because of repudiating one's vow, then it seems that no one is bound to punishment in the future world. But if the swearer should obtain or avoid some such thing in the present world in return for the utterance of a vow to commit or omit some act, then he is bound to punishment in the future world should he repudiate such a vow. It falls to God to judge with certainty regarding the size of the punishment and its temporal duration and whether it is finite or infinite. For I do not consider that one can prove by means of the Holy Scriptures that repudiating a vow binds the swearer to infinite punishment in the condition of the future world; nor can the opposite be demonstrated by the same means. Along the same lines, it ought not to escape our notice that vows uttered for the sake of achieving an advantage or avoiding a disadvantage in the present world are not properly counsels but permissions. Since these may be uttered regarding what is to be done or omitted in the present world on account of obtaining or avoiding something in that same world, they hold one bound to satisfying one's obligations, especially when by means of the vow the object desired has been obtained or likewise an evil has been avoided, on account of the fact that those who voluntarily repudiate such vows without a pressing reason are more greatly bound to punishment in the future world than those who repudiate vows which have been made or uttered for the sake of getting a reward in the future rather than the present world, that is, vows which are uttered by their swearers strictly in the manner of counsels and about matters counselled by divine law. It is a likely conjecture about these strict vows of matters of counsel that in repudiating them, even voluntarily and without a pressing reason, no one is bound to perpetual punishment, nor can this plausibly be supported by Holy Scripture. Nor is the aforementioned opposed to what (as we have indicated above) the Psalmist has said: 'I have rendered to the Lord my vow' nor likewise to what Christ has said: 'Render to Caesar what is Caesar's, and to God what is God's', since nothing more may be concluded from these words, except that the swearer who does not satisfy a vow or who repudiates a vow is bound to some punishment, but is not to be punished eternally for that reason alone.

Chapter 10

[1] There is also a certain other conclusion which some people infer from the already stated power of the sacerdotal keys, namely, that bishops or priests, especially the Roman bishop who is called pope, can on their own authority excommunicate any sinner whomsoever in the present world, unless he has repented of his sin, can deliver him to Satan, and can withhold the divine offices from communities of the faithful who do not obey their mandates or precepts, and can also deny the sacraments and the rest of their spiritual ministrations. Moreover, they wish to ascribe this judgement to numerous passages in Scripture, as is apparent from what is said by them elsewhere.

Explicating this judgement in even greater detail, the Master of the 'Sentences' says in [Book IV,] Distinction 18, Chapter 7 near the end: 'For there is another sort of way of loosing and binding, when someone has been admonished three times according to canonical discipline'.[6] We have quoted this passage in *Defensor pacis*, Discourse II, chapter 6 near the end, and we have neglected to present this here for the sake of brevity. One may assemble in summary the words of judgement which the Master has presented in the same work: if sinners do not wish to repent of the commission of sins by means of the precepts of priests nor to refrain from committing them, then bishops and priests, especially the Roman bishop, can, after the third admonition of their acts, excommunicate them, that is, deprive them of association [*communicatio*] or drive them out in a double sense, namely, first, by denying to them the approval of the church, in which they share by means of the prayers of priests in church which the faithful receive. From this, sinners incur another disadvantage, namely, that there is greater freedom for them to collapse into mortal sin or to sink into other sins in regard to which the devil is conceded a greater power to torment and seduce. On account of this deprivation to sinners of such approval, priests proclaim that sinners are delivering themselves or have delivered themselves to Satan; in fact, priests believe and say that by their individual authority or that of their single assembly they can deprive sinners of association in another sense, namely, civil association, so that others of the faithful should not share with them in other personal, domestic or civil acts, whether in word, agreement or deed; and the rest of the faithful are bound to the observance of this under threat of eternal damnation.

[2] It might seem that the preceding can be imputed on the basis of Holy Scripture. For it may be read that the apostles of Christ, whose successors are believed to be the bishops and presbyters, had exercised such power or authority over their subjects. For this reason, the Apostle says of this in I Corinthians 5[:11]: 'If a brother among you were rapacious or avaricious or worshipped idols', etc., and he adds: 'do not have a meal with him'. Once again, I Corinthians 5[:3–5] states: 'I have already judged him who has done this, delivering his body to Satan for destruction so that his spirit may be cured'. Furthermore, the Apostle says in I or II Timothy [I Timothy 1:19–20]: 'Maintain a good conscience, by which some, not maintaining it, have wrecked their faith, among whom are Hymenaeus and Alexander'' and he adds: 'whom I have handed to Satan, so that they will learn not to commit blasphemy'. Moreover, he says in Titus 3[:10–11]: 'The heretical man is to be given a first and then a second admonition; for he is condemned by his own judgement'. In addition, it is written in II John [10]: 'If someone comes to you, and he has not brought this teaching, do not submit to him nor greet him'. On the basis of these words or writings, it seems that such an authority of excommunication was granted to the apostles and as a consequence to bishops and priests who have succeeded them in sacerdotal office. Yet I remember having read nothing in Scripture

regarding the actual interdiction of communities by Christ or the apostles nor about this pertaining to priests as a result of Holy Scripture, but rather then opposite. Therefore, returning whence the discussion came, we say to those who diligently inspect Holy Scripture that excommunication is, on the one hand, the placing of a certain sinner outside of a community, or, on the other hand, it is the delivering of him to Satan. For what it is to excommunicate or deprive sinners of spiritual association, and likewise what it is to excommunicate sinners from civil association, according to the Master of the 'Sentences' and all priests generally, was stated earlier. But to deliver to Satan in accordance with the truth and meaning of the Apostle and also Scripture is not excommunication in one of the senses mentioned above, but it excludes both. For delivering some sinner to Satan, in accordance with the judgement of the Apostle or Scriptures, is nothing other than supplication and prayer to God on the part of priests and the community of the faithful that the sinner who has earned it may, with the permission or ordination of divine strength, be persecuted by Satan or the Devil in his flesh, but not in his spirit or soul. For this reason, the Apostle says in I Corinthians 5[:3–5]: 'I have already judged him who has done this, you and I meeting together in spirit with the strength of Lord Jesus, to deliver his body to Satan for destruction so that his spirit may be saved'. Behold how the Apostle perceives that deliverance to Satan is done by priests together with the community of the faithful, who invoke the strength of God in order that sinners are persecuted in the flesh or body alone, not in the soul or spirit. And this is also what is said by Augustine in his gloss on the same passage, which we have presented in *Defensor pacis*, Discourse II, chapter 6; and we leave aside its introduction here for the sake of brevity. On account of this, we say, with due reverence to the Master of the 'Sentences' and all others who agree with him, that one cannot demonstrate on the basis of Holy Scripture that anyone can excommunicate a sinner for some transgression or sin, nor that a sinner ought to be deprived of association with, or the approval of, those who pray in church [i.e., priests], in which the faithful share. The opposite is instead demonstrated by Scripture and from the preceding words, in so far as the Apostle says above: 'So that his spirit may be saved'. As the Apostle says in the last chapter of II Corinthians [13:10]: 'For power is not given to us in order to destroy but in order to edify' (namely, souls). Once again, Christ says in Matthew 5[:44]: 'Pray for those who persecute you'. Moreover, Augustine and Prosper says in a certain book on metaphysics: 'There is not to be despair of evil, but prayer that good be done; the whole church seems to pray for this and it prays for infidels, heretics, schismatics and faithless Jews, and also all the rest of the sinners'.[7] On account of this, there neither seems to be nor is any authority on the part of priests to remove from sinners that spiritual approval which they can confer on them by means of their prayers in church. For this work of pastors would not be for the edification of the soul but for its destruction. Chrysostom expresses the same views in his book, 'The Dialogues', and since we have presented passages of this work in *Defensor pacis*, Discourse II, chapters 5 and 9, we do not present them here for the sake of brevity. In addition, this appears to be and is contrary to divine ordination in accordance with the Old Law of Job. For God permitted Satan to persecute Job in his possessions and children and body, yet He always forbade to Satan the persecution of his soul. For this reason, to say that priests or pastors can, either with or without the church of the faithful, deprive sinners of prayers and approval, or can pray to God that they are to be deprived of such things in order that they might be free to rush into mortal sin and that the Devil might be given a great power of tormenting them with regard to their soul or spirit, just as the Master along with those of opinions similar to his seem to maintain, appears to me to be clearly dissonant with the Scriptures. For this reason, it seems that this judgement and those who proclaim it ought to be shunned. Likewise, we also say that no one can demonstrate on the basis of Holy Scripture that priests and bishops either separately or in their single assembly have the power or authority to forbid divine goods to communities of the faithful which are not obedient. For it is written in Matthew 10[:27]: 'What is said to you', etc., 'you must proclaim from the rooftops'. From this it appears clearly that Christ had not wished divine goods to be held back by them or their successors to people, no matter how greatly they rebelled, but rather they were to be spread, just as the example and works of the Saint Peter have confirmed, as is described in the Acts of the Apostles [5:18]. For, when captured and also imprisoned by the rebellious Jews, he did not withdraw divine goods from them nor did he cease proclaiming and promulgating these goods, but on the contrary he proclaimed these same goods to them all the more once he was released from prison.

[3] In addition, I say that excommunicating someone civilly or depriving him of civil association in the manner which was spoken about earlier is not a power of any single bishop or priest, whether communally or separately, nor of the Roman pontiff who is called pope, without the

consent or will of the multitude of the faithful or the greater part [*valentior pars*] standing in their place, whose citizens should prohibit fellowship with sinners, just as is disclosed by the Holy Scripture and for the clear reasons cited in *Defensor pacis*, Discourse II, chapters 6 and 10. For it cannot be demonstrated on the basis of Scripture that this power or authority is owed to priests, but rather the opposite, since in as much as this authority must involve coercion over goods or persons or both, and thus must be applied (however moderately) in this world by the civil power, such authority never pertains to priests, as is proven by the Holy Scriptures cited in *Defensor pacis*, Discourse II, chapters 4, 5, 8 and 10. From this, someone may also recall the primary conclusion of the second discourse of the *Defensor pacis*. For, on the one hand, all the civil kings of the leading men and people would be useless; on the other hand, priests could make individuals and communities subject to them temporally and civilly. For to deprive human beings of civil association in the present world is to deprive them of the necessities of life, such as is the case where a physician or other skilled worker could be prohibited from sharing or associating his task with the rest of the citizens, so that the faithful are bound to observe this out of the necessity of eternal salvation. In that case, priests or their single assembly could inflict upon any sinner whomsoever the punishment of exile and also remove his wealth and income by which the faithful Christian ought to sustain his family along with himself in the present world – a view which is dissonant with all of the Holy Scriptures cited earlier. For this reason, one can and should infer from the preceding that there is no power or authority of priests to excommunicate individual believers either spiritually or civilly, that is, to deprive them of spiritual approval or of civil association, nor to interdict communities of believers or to deny the divine offices to them. And I say, furthermore, that a bishop or priest, whomsoever he may be, sins mortally by interdicting or refusing such instruction as the celebration of the mass or preaching, and other similar functions, and whatever divine or spiritual ministration the people faithful to Christ wish to hear and desire to receive. For this reason, the Apostle says in I Corinthians 9[:16]: 'Woe to me if I should not preach the Gospel, for necessity presses down upon me', by reason of the office, namely, episcopal or priestly, entrusted to him. Moreover, surrendering some sinner to Satan is not the same as excommunicating him, and once again, believers are not bound out of necessity of eternal salvation to obey or comply with the precepts of excommunications or divine interdicts of priests or their single assembly.

[4] Regarding what has previously been presented by them on the basis of Scripture, we can abrogate their statements, first, because what Scripture says about this is perhaps a matter of counsel rather than precept. And should it be the case that this is a precept according to Scripture, from which it would be criminal to deviate, I say that such authority of prescribing or otherwise harassing rebels belongs not solely to priests or their single assembly, but this authority or power belongs to the community of the faithful or its greater part, by which the sinner ought to be excluded on account of his crime, just as is plainly revealed in *Defensor pacis*, Discourse II, chapter 6 and may be examined in the same work by those who are interested. The previously presented authorities of Scripture, the Apostle as well as John, should be understood in this way, for if it were to be a precept, then it is directed to the multitude or community of the faithful, whether civil or domestic, as is evident from their letters and writings and the expositions of saints, which we have introduced above.

[5] In regard to the delivery of someone to Satan, it may be said (in accordance with the gloss on the above words of I Corinthians 5[:3–5]: 'I have already judged him', etc., 'delivering his body to Satan for destruction', etc.) that the Apostle has possession of this virtue or gift – in that Satan will persecute in body, that is, corporeally, those whom the Apostle has prayed to be persecuted on account of committing crimes – as a result of divine ordination or power. For he does not have such power or authority from God in so far as he is a man, or in so far as he is a bishop or priest, but he has this gift as a result of his spiritual merits. For if he has this in so far as he is a bishop or priest, then all the bishops and priests who succeeded him and the other apostles would have such power, whereas the opposite is and has up to this point been confirmed. It remains to turn our attention, however, to whether it is expedient to separate heretics from, or deprive them of, the fellowship of believers and by whom this authority is possessed. And in regard to separating heretics and other infidels from the fellowship of believers. I say that they are to be shunned, especially in connection with domestic or social relations, or cohabitation or conversation, concerning those matters which pertain to the preservation of the rituals of the faith, especially after a first and a second admonition is given to them along the lines of the Apostle's counsel, lest they taint the remaining believers, although non-heretical infidels are not to be shunned in this way. For this reason, the Apostle says in I Corinthians 10[:27]: 'If some infidel has invited you to have a

meal, eat from that which is placed before you, questioning nothing on account of conscience'. Therefore, fellowship or a close relationship with infidels is not prohibited by Scripture, nor may it be objected that the Apostle says: 'You cannot plough together with infidels' (II Corinthians 6:14]. For this is to be understood in regard to belief and the observance of the rituals of the faith, rather than in regard to other domestic or civil intercourse, just as has been shown above, and once again since the Apostle says that 'the unbelieving man is saved by a faithful wife', etc. [I Corinthians 7:14].

[6] The matter of who possesses the authority to separate heretics by compulsion or restraint through the punishment of persons or their property is discussed adequately by us in *Defensor pacis*, Discourse II, chapter 10, in as much as this power belongs not to priests, nor to a single assembly of them, but to the secular rulers or human legislator. For this reason, all of the temporal goods of heretics do not revert to priests, but to the aforementioned legislators or rulers.

Chapter 11

[1] It remains to turn our attention to whether some plenitude of power in the management of spiritual affairs pertains to the Roman pontiff, who is called pope, to a greater extent than other apostles or priests as a result of his succession from Saint Peter, and whether Peter possessed this to the same extent over the other apostles by means of an immediate concession to him from God or Christ.

For it may be read that Christ had possessed such a plenitude of power, in so far as Matthew 28[:18] says: 'All power in heaven and on earth is given to me'. Therefore, just as Saint Peter was the successor to Christ, and the Roman pontiffs, who are called popes, were and are the successors to Saint Peter, as they commonly say, so it seems that Peter, as successor to Christ, and the Roman pontiffs, as his successors, must have the previously mentioned plenitude of power.

We say, however, that Christ uniquely was joined out of two natures, namely, divine and human. For this reason, He was truly both God and man, and consequently certain things could pertain to Christ in so far as he was God, namely, fashioning the world, creating all visible and invisible entities and also performing supernatural miracles in the present world, and moreover, bringing or giving divine law to mankind for the sake of its condition in the future world and restraining transgressors by coercive judgement in accordance with it and saving those who observe it. For this reason, James 4[:12], which we presented above, says: 'There is a single legislator and judge, He who can condemn and deliver'. In accordance with this consideration, what is written in Revelation 19[:16] is validated with regard to Christ: 'King of Kings and Lord of Lords'. In accordance with this consideration, likewise, none of the apostles nor any human being could or would be able to be the successor to Christ. For this reason, Augustine in *De verbis Domini*, his tenth sermon concerning Matthew, speaks thus: 'Learn from me, not because of making the world, nor creating all visible and invisible entities, nor performing miracles in this world, and raising the dead, but learn from me because I am gentle and of humble heart'.[8] These latter qualities pertain to his humanity, and for that reason certain other things also pertain to Christ in so far as He was a man, namely, that He was born of woman and lived under the law, as the Apostle says: 'When the fullness of time came, God sent His only son, born of woman, living under law' [Galatians 4:4] and likewise was circumcised, was consumed, thirsted, suffered, died corporeally, was resurrected from the dead, along with many other similar things which we have omitted from presenting in this list on account of brevity, since they are known by means of Scripture and by everyone.

[2] Therefore, all apostles and bishops or presbyters, who succeeded the apostles, are successors to Christ in so far as He was a man and a human priest. But in so far as Christ was God, or in so far as He was God and man simultaneously, no apostle or human being succeeds or can succeed Him, and in virtue of this dual nature Christ was given all power in heaven and on earth, or a plenitude of power in accordance with His divinity alone. This plenitude of power can never and never has been able to pertain to the successors of the apostles, since none of these has or had a duality of natures, namely, human and also divine, joined into one.

[3] It is now necessary to turn our attention to the remaining matter of whether Saint Peter was the sole successor of Christ and had some power which the rest of the apostles did not have on account of authority conceded to him immediately from God or Christ, and through the preceding institution of which he became head of the church.

For it seems to some people and they say that Saint Peter had authority in spiritual matters and perhaps in temporal or civil affairs over the rest of the apostles, and that he was head of the church, and consequently that the Roman church is to be the principal one and head of the other churches on account of authority handed or conceded to him immediately from God or Christ. Although it might seem that one can be persuaded of this on the basis of many passages in Holy Scripture, we have nevertheless omitted presenting these, since they are scattered and adequately presented elsewhere, as will be seen below. Moreover, we wish to adduce and to add to the aforementioned passages of Scripture the arguments of those persons who thrive by reinforcing the conclusion mentioned immediately above. For as they declare and assert, the entire Christian church has believed and proclaimed that doctrine up to now, and believes and proclaims it still, but the universal Church cannot err, they say. From this it follows that Saint Peter had the aforementioned priority over the apostles and that the Roman church has it over the rest of the churches, in the way which was stated earlier, from which they also infer that Roman bishops have this priority over all the rest of the priests and bishops. We say, however, that the universal Church of Christian believers can speak about those things which are to be believed in accordance with Holy Scripture on account of the necessity of eternal salvation, for example, those which are articles of faith and other analogous precepts in accordance with Scripture or following by necessity from it; or the universal Church can speak about certain matters which pertain to the proper observance of ecclesiastical ritual, which are convenient or expedient for peaceful human fellowship and a tranquil state in the present world, and also which are arranged in order that happiness in the future world may be achieved and punishment or misery may be avoided. And once again, the universal Church can issue its commands about the aforementioned matters in accordance with certain widely known and customary practices, according to which these directives have proceeded from the decree of perhaps one or a few men of authority and in this way they are to be spread to the others, or the universal Church can speak about the preceding matters according to the sure and binding determinations made by a general council of the church or of all faithful Christians mentioned above.

If some have reasonable doubts about those matters which are to be believed in accordance with Holy Scripture out of necessity of eternal salvation, then the universal Church is to make a declaration about them by means of a determination or deliberation made in the general council mentioned above, which has been properly convoked, organized and concluded. The role of the general council is to declare firmly those things which ought to be believed by all faithful Christians out of the necessity of eternal salvation, since such truths are certain and immutable, because they proceed from precisely the same spirit of canonical or Holy Scripture, just as is stated adequately in *Defensor pacis*, Discourse II, chapter 19, where it may be examined by those who are interested. If something is declared about such matters by the universal Church mentioned above in accordance with certain widely known and customary practices which have arisen, by means of the decree of one or a few celebrated men without the deliberation of the above mentioned general council, namely, some modern or ancient person or persons who are or were saintly and blessed, I say that such decrees can be believed by all the faithful in accordance with the widely known or customary practices already stated, yet not out of necessity of eternal salvation. And in this way I say that the universal Church speaks and can speak according to the customary and widely known practices which have or could have arisen with regard to the Roman bishop and his assembly [*collegio*] of clerics, on the grounds that Saint Peter and the Roman church have possessed the said priority over all the remaining bishops and priests and churches generally, regardless of whether this occurred as the result of believing it to be the meaning of Scripture or perhaps out of some pious intention, so that Christian churches might be more readily conducted to the observance of unity, and that other churches might be more readily induced to obey a superior. For this reason, I do not recall that I have read in Scripture or in something that follows by necessity from Scripture that the said priority of Saint Peter or the Roman church was conceded immediately by God or Christ, on account of which it is not necessary to believe in these claims out of necessity of eternal salvation, since they are neither articles of faith nor precepts of Scripture. For in fact the faithful redeemed by Christ, who was and is always the head of the church, can be saved without believing that Saint Peter was chief and head over the others. If some priority pertains or had pertained to Saint Peter over the apostles, or to the Roman church over the others, since Saint Peter, who had enjoyed greater reverence among the apostles, occupied that same episcopacy, I say that the priority of Saint Peter had proceeded from the election or consent of the remaining apostles, just as is stated in Anacletus;[9] this passage is presented in *Defensor pacis*, Discourse II, chapter 16, and we have omitted to repeat it for the sake of brevity. Thus, we say that the priority of the church of Rome over the others has proceeded from its already mentioned suitability or from tradition or from the constitution of the general council of faithful Christians or from the human and supreme legislator, although such priority might on grounds of suitability seem to be owed to the church of Jerusalem, which is indeed unique, since the foremost pastor, namely, Christ, resided there as if its bishop and the single most famous of the apostles, along with two other very famous apostles, also guided it and exercised the pastoral office there earlier than in Rome. If the universal Church declared something about these matters, which involve only the rituals of the church or the tranquillity or peace of the fellowship and condition of human beings, as we have said earlier, which are established in a general council, then we say that these same declarations ought to be observed by the faithful. Yet believers are not bound out of necessity of eternal salvation to believe these declarations to be true, or likewise expedient, for any time whatsoever, since such decrees may be loosened and can be revoked totally or in part by the same council whenever the times or other conditions make it suitable. And for that reason we have said that such priority of the Roman bishop or Roman church is conceded rather by the supreme faithful human legislator, and this has already been conceded in fact and in right, in so far as it is supported by authentic human documents.

Chapter 12

[1] Furthermore, since we have spoken about the general council, it ought to be examined who the human legislator might be and, once again, from which and what kind of provinces the above mentioned general councils have to be constituted and created.

Regarding the first of these topics whose examination is to be undertaken here, we say that the supreme human legislator, especially from the time of Christ up to the present time, and perhaps for some time beforehand, was and is and ought to be the community [*universitas*] of human beings who ought to be subject to the precepts of coercive laws, or their greater part, in each region and province. And since this power or authority was transferred by the communites of the provinces, or their greater part, to the Roman people, in accordance with their exceeding virtue, the Roman people have and had the authority to legislate over all of the world's provinces. If this people had transferred its authority to legislate to its rulers, then its rulers may likewise be said to possess such power, so that the authority or power of legislation (namely, of the

Roman people and its rulers) has endured for so long a time and ought reasonably to endure, until such a time as it might be revoked by the communities of the provinces from the Roman people or by the Roman people from its ruler. And we maintain that such powers are duly revoked or revocable when the communities of the provinces, by themselves or by their syndics, or the Roman people, have been duly congregated and they, or their greater part, have performed deliberations about such revocation, just as we have asserted and demonstrated in *Defensor pacis*, Discourse I, chapter 12.

[2] For in this way, the preceding power of legislation has been gathered by the Roman people and ruler, just as is evident from the proof of the histories. Divine Scripture also attests to this. For as is evident in *Defensor pacis*, Discourse II, chapters 4 and 5 from the words of Christ and the Apostle Paul, the Roman people and ruler had the preceding power and exercised a just monarchy over the whole of the world's provinces. Consequently, Christ as well as the Apostles Paul and Peter (in the second chapter of his first letter [I Peter 2:13–15]) testify that everyone is admonished to obey and subject themselves to the already mentioned power, and also to obey the above mentioned people as well as their ruler under threat of eternal damnation, for which reason Christ says: 'Render to Caesar what is Caesar's' [Matthew 22:21] and Paul says in Romans 13[:1–2]: 'Everyone is to be subject to the higher powers', etc., and 'he who resists the powerful resists what God ordains; and he who resists Him acquires damnation for himself', namely, in eternity. And once again, [I] Timothy [2:1–2] says: 'First, I beg that prayers', etc., 'be made for kings and those who are on high'. Moreover, Titus [3:1] says: 'Admonish them', namely, those who were previously mentioned, 'to be subject to princes and powerful persons'; furthermore, Saint Peter says in the above text: 'Be subject', etc., 'whether to the king as a superior or to governors sent by Him', namely, God, 'in order to avenge wrongdoers and praise those who do good, because this is the will of God' [I Peter 2:13–15].

[3] It is certain that all the powers that were wielded in those times by the authority of the Romans were wielded justly, rather than tyrannically, for otherwise Christ and the apostles would not have admonished everyone else in the preceding passages of their obligation to subject themselves to government, not even objecting that the Roman people and their rulers and all other rulers throughout the whole world instituted by them were infidels. For this reason, the Acts of the Apostles 25[:10] also

says: 'I appeal to Caesar; I stand before his tribunal; it is appropriate for me to be judged there'. Nor was it unknown to the apostles that Caesar and the governors who were then present in Jerusalem by his authority were infidels. Nor may it be objected, as some people say, that the lordship [*dominium*] of the Roman people as well as their rulers had been violent and had originated out of violence. For although the Roman people sometimes coerced certain wicked peoples who willed to live unjustly and barbarously, still it did not subject the whole of the provinces or their greater parts by means of violence. On the contrary, many provinces, observing the benevolence of Roman rule and wishing to live tranquilly and peacefully, elected by their own volition to subject themselves to and be protected by the above mentioned Roman people and their rulers. For this reason, it is written in I Maccabees 8 about Judas Maccabee and his brothers and the whole Jewish people that they subjected themselves voluntarily to the friendship or rulership of the Romans. A similar pattern may be ascribed to the rest of the world's provinces and may be discovered, as we have said above, from recitation of the chronicles or histories written by those of meritorious faith, and also from the more full and certain confirmation of the preceding testimony of Christ and the apostles in Holy Scripture.

[4] In regard to the remaining issue – namely, by whom a general council of faithful Christians ought to be constituted and created – it is discussed by us in *Defensor pacis*, Discourse II, chapter 21, and so is the question of who is authorized to congregate or call it and of the means by which such a council ought to be drawn to a close. It seems to be something additional to what has already been said that a general council can and ought never to be called unless the whole faithful Greek church has been duly called to it; this is demonstrated by the four principal councils: Nicea, Ephesus, Constantinople and Chalcedon. The bishops and prelates and priests of the Greeks had been duly called to these councils by Constantine I and the other rulers succeeding him. For the Church of Christ or the faithful existed first among the Greeks rather than among the Latins. For this reason, the Apostle in Romans 1[:16] set them in greeting before the Latins, in so far as he said: 'First the Jews and then Greece'. For the Greeks, according to the statements of many learned teachers of the Old Law (and the Master of the 'Sentences' seems almost to incline towards this judgement), did not differ in reality and in true belief from the Latins concerning the procession of the Holy Spirit, but only with regard to some superficial matters of wording. For this

reason, they ought not to be judged schismatics, even though the Roman bishop and his coterie of brothers or cardinals might seem to say so, even to little avail. This should be rectified by the Roman people and ruler, and both parties – Greeks as well as Latins – ought to be called to a council, just as Constantine I had done, so that by means of this same council such apparent schism or dissension would be removed and the Church of Christ would be restored to unity in judgement as well as words.

[5] As to whether a general council, duly called together and drawn to a close in order to explain doubtful matters in Holy Scripture which all the faithful are to believe out of necessity of eternal salvation, can err when it is duly set up, the answer is negative as is adequately determined by us in *Defensor pacis*, Discourse II, chapter 19. Nor may it be objected by means of the false reasoning which some have inferred from positions and distinctions which have been presented that a given person can err in doubtful matters concerning the faith and that what is the case about individuals is therefore true for all. For this inference is defective on account of its form, as we have said, since although in its meaning the distinction arises in regard to singulars, nevertheless it is falsely predicated of composites, and this also appears evident in other instances. For it does not follow that if each person cannot haul a boat apart from others, or perform some other similar action, this same action cannot be performed by a multitude of persons joined together. So likewise or analogously, a multitude of the faithful is joined together in a council. For by each one listening to the others, their minds are reciprocally stimulated to the consideration of that truth at which not one of them would arrive if he existed apart or separately from the others. And once again, this seems to be or has been divinely ordained and was practised in the early church. For this reason, it may be read in Acts 15 [:6 and 28] that in regard to certain doubtful matters concerning the faith, the apostles and elders, congregating together with the whole church which was at Jerusalem, proceeded in their deliberations according to the guiding power of the Holy Spirit, just as the same Scripture testifies when it is said: 'It appeared to the Holy Spirit and to us', etc. On the basis of the preceding it may be supposed that the general council of the faithful mentioned above is to represent [*representare*] the congregation in a similar and valid manner. For this reason, 'I am with you until the end of the world', Christ says to the apostles in Matthew 28[:20]. What has been said is to be believed firmly about the apostles as well as their

successors and all of the faithful, because it is well known that the apostles themselves died long before the end of the world.

Chapter 13

[1] It remains to enquire into and treat certain problems or questions in addition to our earlier topics. The first of these is: whether there is any reason on account of which a male and female of the human species who are said to be in wedlock, or a husband and wife whose combination one is commonly accustomed to call marriage, cannot be joined together in such marriage, and by whose authority this can be impeded. And, on the other hand, if such a marriage as already stated was consummated, can or ought they to be separated from marriage to one another for some reason and by whose authority may this be done? A second problem is also connected to this: whether some degree of consanguinity, which is an impediment to legitimate matrimony, can or ought to be dispelled by dispensation.

[2] Consequently, turning to the subject to be explained, the following points ought to be noted. The combination of male with female in the human species, and their reciprocal relations for the sake of joining together, may be natural, of course, just as even other animals are naturally inclined to it on account of procreation and propagation, and by means of it they may share in the immortality and eternality of divinity according to the way in which it is possible for them, as is said, in so far as they are natural creatures. Still, because the human genus lives by art and reason, the combination of wedlock mentioned above, if allowed to be made and dissolved for given reasons and in given ways, is and was up to this point instituted according to many rules or statutes and certain customs. But since there are various types and modes of laws or statutes, some of which are and are called human, some divine (which are by common custom named 'sects'), the preceding combination was and is ordained in various ways and by many means. With regard to the description of the many different kinds of laws which may exist, and the fact that among them some are affirmative precepts and some are negative (which are called prohibitions), and that others (named permissions) are neither affirmative precepts nor prohibitions, such descriptions and differentiations are discussed adequately by us in *Defensor pacis*, Discourse II, chapter 12 and near the beginning of the current tract. Yet omitting for the present discussion and treatment of the combination of

male with female, which was already called marriage, in accordance with other laws or sects, it is our intention to treat the problems set out previously concerning marriage solely in connection with the Christian sect and as regards its disposition by human and divine laws according to that sect. For to the extent that such a determination is achieved, the problems or questions mentioned above could likewise or analogously be resolved in connection with other sects. And so, taking up our intention again, it is necessary first to describe what marriage is according to Christian ritual and common estimation. For marriage in its proper signification means the combination of a male with a female of the human species accomplished by the consent in person of both people, expressed voluntarily rather than under compulsion by means of words or gestures, and who are of the prescribed age. This consent obligates both of the wedded parties to live together and to surrender themselves corporeally to carnal coupling for the procreation of descendants. Such sexual desire is to be quenched whenever this might be duly required of one party by the other for an uninterrupted duration as long as they are alive. To describe marriage in this way, one must treat problems beyond the topic itself in order that the evidence related is certain and complete. It is consequently necessary to notice that those faithful to Christ live and are ruled under two laws, human and divine.

[3] Law properly speaking is a coercive precept concerning the commission or omission of human acts under threat of punishment to be inflicted upon transgressors. Divine law is a coercive precept made by God immediately on account of the pursuit of ends in the future world and under threat of punishment to be inflicted upon transgressors only in that same world rather than in the present one. But human law is a coercive precept proceeding immediately from human will or deliberation, on account of the pursuit of immediate ends in the present world and under threat of punishment to be inflicted upon transgressors in that realm alone. Equally, it is necessary to notice that in regard to either one of the laws, some are affirmative precepts, namely, about what is to be done, while some are negative, about what is to be omitted or not done, which are called prohibitions. Moreover, some are permissions for action or inaction, which are not classified as either affirmative or negative precepts, and are sometimes called counsels in the case of divine law. The permissions just mentioned are a more general sort of precept, since all precepts about action are permissions to act, but the converse is not always true. Likewise, too, all prohibition of action is permission not to

act, although not the converse of this. Also, it is understood that matters are similar with regard to human laws in connection with affirmative precepts, prohibitions and permissions, but are different as concerns punishment, since on the basis of divine law, precepts and prohibitions bind transgressors to eternal punishment, whereas transgressors against human law are bound to the temporal punishment of this world, without punishment in the future. Once again, it is also to be noticed that with regard to either one of the laws already mentioned, the terms 'prescribe' and 'prohibit' can have two meanings or significations: namely, first, that the term 'prescribe' or 'prohibit' may be understood as the act of prescribing or as the precept proceeding from the prescriber, speaking in an active fashion; in the other way, the preceding terms are understood not as the act of prescribing – he who prescribes or gives orders – but rather as the act or work of those who have been given a precept, in a passive fashion. In this way, it is commonly said that the slave has performed the precept of the lord, when he does it or omits to do it, because a precept to act or refrain from action has been given to him by his lord, for instance, to prepare a horse, pour the wine and other such matters of service. This sort of precept or prohibition signifies or conveys the same thing as that which is commanded [*imperatum*], in contrast with the active sense of commanding [*imperium*] or the act of giving a precept, since a slave does not perform such an act, in so far as he is a slave, but only a lord does so.

[4] Furthermore, it is to be noticed that affirmative as well as negative precepts of divine law, and also permissions which are called counsels, are, and are called, spiritual [*spiritualia*]. This is because, first, they were instituted and handed down immediately by the Holy Spirit, just as Saint Ambrose says about the Apostle's words in I Corinthians 9: 'I say that the evangelical law and the words of God are spiritual; grace is also perhaps spiritual, since it is a gift of the Holy Spirit which is attained and exists in the souls of the Christian faithful by the evangelical words mentioned above'.[10] Second, such precepts are also said to be spiritual since they are established and handed down in order to animate the human spirit or soul and on account of eternal happiness. These are called the precepts and prohibitions of divine law, speaking actively. Certain others are not essentially spiritual, but they have taken over the vocabulary from certain spiritual affairs because they were and are ordained by human beings for the sake of carrying out or administering the aforementioned spiritual affairs, as for instance the persons and

bodies of priests, also the house of prayer called the church (in a certain sense thereof), also the vessels, clothing, books and other sorts of instruments ordained by men on account of divine worship; also fasting, alms-giving and other sorts of acts, and all human works in regard to divine and spiritual matters, and connected to or on account of spiritual affairs, which men carry out as though commanded. Examples of all of these, since they are widely known, are omitted for the sake of the brevity of the discussion.

[5] Analogously, according to human law, there are also active precepts, prohibitions and permissions, and other similar commands, which are called temporal [*temporalia*] because they are established and handed down immediately by men. And once again, such temporal matters, so called because they are limited or confined in time, were and are established on account of life in this world. In addition, the following points should be noted. Active precepts and prohibitions and counsels according to divine law differ from precepts according to human law, since these are established and ordained by another legislator and on account of other ends, and also under threat of other types and lengths of punishment to be inflicted upon those who transgress them. Still, those persons, actions or deeds subject to what is prescribed or commanded by either law can and are to be identical in all cases, or at least in most instances, such as, for example, not committing theft or homicide or robbery or fraud or false testimony, and other similar acts which divine as well as human law order not to be done.

[6] This is similarly the case for affirmative precepts as well, such as returning a loan or deposit. Once again, the persons to whom, and likewise the acts about which, either sort of law prescribes can be the same, in regard to temporal as well as spiritual affairs, precisely as their actions can be. For in connection with temporal affairs and what relates to temporal matters, something can be done or omitted licitly or illicitly according or contrary to the precepts of divine as well as human law by priests, bishops or presbyters, and it can be justly corrected or punished in the condition of the present as well as the future world, namely, they may be restrained as transgressors by means of punishment whenever they are guilty; this has been proven by previous examples. Thus, also, in connection with spiritual affairs and what relates to spiritual affairs, regardless of what they are called, something can be done or omitted licitly or illicitly by the aforementioned persons and their acts, for instance, preaching or teaching heresies, baptising an animal or someone

who is violent, making sacrifices to demons in order that they might make certain sacrilegious prophesies. Also, the commission of other crimes, such as looting or stealing vessels, books, clothing and the rest of the corporeal instruments of service in divine worship and other such acts, is justly to be punished in the present world and in the next by means of penalties against their persons or property in accordance with both laws, namely, divine and human, although in a different manner, and with different penalties and judges, and at different places and times, just has been said and will be discussed once again below. Furthermore, it is also to be noticed that if divine law prescribes something to be done or omitted the doing or omitting of which is not prescribed by human law, but rather the opposite is prescribed or permitted, then one ought to observe the precepts of divine law, condemning or dismissing human law or its contrary precept or permission since the precepts of divine law contain infallible truth, whereas human law does not encompass this.

[7] And once again, since divine precepts bind transgressors to eternal punishment, whereas human precepts bind them to temporal or finite punishment which is to be feared less by human beings, it is furthermore to be noticed that each of the already mentioned laws has its own and distinct immediate legislator and judges, as was stated above. And moreover, since there are two sorts of judges, only one is a learned teacher and also perhaps a practitioner in regard to certain matters, just as is evident in every discipline; this is also written by a famous philosopher named Aristotle, who says that 'each one is a good judge of those matters which he knows and he judges these well',[11] for example, a physician about health and illness.

The other sort of judge is properly called a ruler, to whom is handed authority and is given coercive power over transgressors against the law by the constraints of punishment. This is indeed the judge in accordance with human law about whom the Apostle has said that 'it is not without reason that he bears the sword', that is, he has coercive and military power, 'since he is a minister of God, avenger in wrath against him who does evil' [Romans 13:4]. It is also the case that he need not be conspicuously learned in human law. Moreover, according to divine law, there is a coercive judge, about whom Saint James said in his Letter [4:12]: 'There is a single legislator and judge, He who can condemn and deliver', namely, Christ.

[8] Consequently, in as much as this may be taken as true and recognized, it may be said that according to divine law, the legislator and

coercive judge on the basis of it is Christ, in accordance with what was said above by Saint James. For the divine law or New Testament was disclosed by Him, through the mouths of the apostles as well as many of the other saints. For this reason, the Apostle says: 'Have you found proof that He who speaks in me is Christ' [II Corinthians 13:3]? And Saint Peter in his Letters says that 'no prophecy is asserted by the human spirit, but men who speak the holy words of God are inspired by the Holy Spirit' [II Peter 1:21]. Moreover, this legislator has decided to be a judge of transgressors on the basis of this law and to restrain them by means of punishment in the future world only, rather than in the present one. For this reason, the Scripture says: 'When the Son of Man arrives upon His glorious throne, you will sit and upon twelve thrones you will be judges of the twelve tribes of Israel' [Matthew 19:28], which will be in the future world, just as Scripture clearly proclaims and all the expositions of it by the saints reveal.

[9] Once again, there are other judges according to divine law, those called learned teachers whom nothing prevents from being numerous, and whose acts or works are administered or performed in accordance with divine law, yet who have no coercive authority or power from Christ or divine law to restrain anyone in the present world for something done or omitted by means of some punishment of their persons or property. For this reason, Christ in the last book of Matthew [28:19] calls such judges 'teachers', in so far as He says of them in the persons of the apostles: 'Go teach all nations, baptising them', etc. And it is said by the Prophet Malachi [2:7]: 'The lips of priests preserve knowledge, and the law is to be sought from their mouths'; and these bishops or presbyters are the judges called learned teachers. The aforementioned judges lack and ought to lack the coercive authority and power to constrain anyone by means of punishment, just as was previously stated, since Christ willed Himself to lack such authority in the present world in so far as He was a man, in as much as He said: 'My kingdom is not of this world', in regard to authority; 'if my kingdom were of this world, my servants would fight at any rate', etc. [John 18:36], in regard to military or coercive power. And once again, He responds plainly to the person who sought after his share of an inheritance: 'Man, who instituted me judge or distributor over you?' [Luke 12:14], or as He might say, it does not pertain to me to exercise such judgement between you and your brother. In this way, also, He willed the apostles to lack such coercive authority and power and, in their persons, all bishops and presbyters who succeeded the apostles and

all whom in turn succeeded them, in so far as He was a human priest (since in so far as He was God, no human succeeds or could succeed Him), in as much as He said to them: 'Kings are lords of their peoples, yet you are not this way' [Luke 22:25–26]. 'It is clear that the apostles are forbidden to be lords', as Bernard says.[12] In the same way, too, have all the saints and approved teachers harmoniously understood and explicated the Holy Scripture; and they have expressed the same view by their own judgements that the Apostle realized and stated – that he did not have any power to coerce anyone with regard to spiritual affairs, much less temporal affairs – as he said in [II] Corinthians [1:24]: 'We will not be lord over your faith', words about which Ambrose as well as Chrysostom have spoken clearly and judged harmoniously. Ambrose remarks: '"*We will not be lord over your faith*," that is, because your faith is not to endure lordship or coercion, since it is voluntary rather than necessary'.[13] Likewise, Chrysostom comments: 'In the church it is necessary to direct people towards what is better not by coercion but by acquiescence; that admirable man', namely, the Apostle, 'was actually thinking this when he said in Corinthians: "*We will not be lord over your faith*"'; and additionally, Chrysostom says: 'For the power or authority of judgement was not given to law by us', namely, bishops or presbyters, 'in order that we might restrain men from wantonness, nor, if it was given, would we have the power when he might exercise it, since our God', namely, Christ, 'is a rewarder of those who banish sin not by necessity', that is, force, 'but who avert it by their own volition'.[14] In these words, Chrysostom also assumes that all coercive power in the present world is given by laws or rulers, as Hugh of St Victor also says in the second book of *De sacramentis*. For he says that 'although ecclesiastics', that is, ecclesiastical persons, bishops or presbyters, 'may exercise coercive jurisdiction, namely, over secular persons, still that which they exercise they know themselves to have from royal power'.[15] Therefore, any coercive authority or power whatsoever in the present world, especially that of a bishop or presbyter, derives not from divine but from human law. For this reason, Chrysostom adds to the aforementioned words: 'If a man would be diverted from true faith, the priest should lean towards exhorting him with great patience and industry, because he cannot draw the erring person back by such force, but he must try to persuade him that he ought to turn back to the true faith, from which he previously moved away'.[16] All the saintly expositors and learned teachers have also equally thought the same thing about Holy Scripture, copious passages of which – omitted for the sake of brevity – can be seen, for those interested, in the *Defensor pacis*, and also previously in this tract of ours. Likewise, there is also, in accordance with human law, a legislator, such as the community of citizens or their greater part, or the supreme Roman ruler who is called emperor. And there is a coercive judge in accordance with the same law, such as the community or ruler already mentioned, or one or more persons to whom the community or ruler has given coercive authority and power to coerce transgressors against human law by the punishment of persons or their property in the present world. Bishops or presbyters, or other ministers of spiritual affairs, whether communally or separately, are on no account human legislators in their own right, although perhaps they participate in accordance with the fact that they exist as some part of the civic body [*civitas*], according to what is clearly demonstrated by certain human reason and Holy Scripture in *Defensor pacis*, Discourse I, chapters 12 and 13, and Discourse II, chapters 4 and 5, and what was already elaborated consistently above.

[10] And there are other judges in accordance with human law who are called legal experts or learned teachers, and who have no coercive authority in their own right to restrain anyone in the present world by some punishment of persons or their property in order that something licit may be done or something illicit omitted, but have authority only in order that certain things may be taught or proclaimed in accordance with human law, in the same way that bishops or presbyters have authority in accordance with divine law. On account of looking at the matter more clearly, it may be realized that a two-fold uncertainty can occur about human acts or works touching on divine matters and also about divine matters of a similar sort touching on temporal affairs and what relates to temporal concerns, and as a consequence I will raise queries or questions because of the necessity of considering these uncertainties.

Chapter 14

[1] One such uncertainty and question is: whether there exists a precept or prohibition in regard to a particular action or deed, the commission or omission of which one is contemplating, that is, whether the deed is licit or illicit, according to divine law as well as human law. The other query or question about which there can be uncertainty on the

basis of the foregoing is: whether such actions or deeds were in fact done or omitted by someone.

[2] To respond to the first uncertainty, question or query, either judging it or determining it by judgement pertains to the learned teachers or doctrinal judges having such authority, of which sort are and should be all bishops and presbyters according to divine law, as was revealed above; and the Apostle says in [1] Timothy 3[:2]: 'A bishop ought to be a learned teacher'. Moreover, in regard to human law, this authority or judgement pertains to legal experts or learned teachers of human law. For it is their duty to know, to teach and, if necessary, to proclaim which and of what sort are precepts, prohibitions and permissions according to the aforementioned laws, and also what human action is licit and illicit, or to be done or omitted. Responding likewise about such matters when questions have been raised in this regard, all are lacking the coercive authority or power to compel anyone to avoid or to do something by punishment in the present world, as we indicated above. Just as physicians have learning and practical experience in accordance with the precepts of the medical arts in order that the health of the body may be conserved or its well-being recovered, so they cannot compel anyone to observe a suitable diet, nor to avoid a harmful one, by imposing some punishment on the persons or property of patients. In this way, also, priests who are physicians of souls cannot restrain anyone on the basis of Scripture by punishment in the present world. And consequently, although it is allowed for priests to urge or make regulations or exhortations in regard to good morals and works to be done, still such regulations are not and cannot be called laws, but rather instructions or rules. Nor ought their judgements on the basis of such regulations regarding human action to be called jurisdiction or public justice (*forum*), because such names are properly speaking appropriate in accordance with their first and true meaning.

[3] The preceding judgement, since it is general, can be made equally in ignorance of the persons about whose acts there is uncertainty or question. The second uncertainty, question or query which can occur in connection with the aforementioned human action or work – namely, whether some action or deed was in fact done by omission or commission by someone – pertains to the judgement of the ruling coercive judge who is authorized to restrain transgressors of the law by the punishment of persons and their property in the present or future world.

[4] In regard to divine law and in the future world only, not in this one,

such a judge is Christ alone, and perhaps with Him will be the twelve apostles, about whom it may be read in Scripture: 'When the Son of Man arrives upon His glorious throne, you will sit and upon twelve thrones you will be judges of the twelve tribes of Israel' [Matthew 19:28]. In regard to human law, such a judge is the ruler on the authority of the human legislator, who has coercive power to restrain transgressors of the human law by punishment of their persons and property in the present world only, not the future one. In fact, in order that His coercive judgement may be exercised, the judge in accordance with divine law does not need to investigate the truth by means of evidence, nor to restrain witnesses in court for the truth to be spoken, 'since all things are exposed and open to His eyes' [Hebrews 4:13], nor does He need the sword or the weapons of the servants of coercive power so that His judgement may be executed, since 'He spoke, and it was done' [Psalm 33:9]. This is not so with the coercive human ruler, since he can be ignorant of whether or not someone charged with or accused of an instance of an illicit action has committed it. And therefore it is necessary for litigants as well as witnesses to speak in court, and for him to compel them by armed force, since perhaps they would not come on account of a simple summons to them, especially the accused and those who might consider that punishment was due to them.

Chapter 15

[1] From what has already been set forth, therefore, one can prepare a response to the principal question, namely, which judge is authorized to decide with regard to the dissolution of a marriage requested by either or both spouses. If there would be an uncertainty or question about whether the marriage in question may be licit or prohibited by divine law for some reason, the authority of judging with regard to it and responding is the responsibility of bishops or presbyters and learned teachers of divine law appointed for such purposes in accordance with those honourable laws and customs of regions which are not incompatible with divine law. For it belongs to them to know the precepts and prohibitions and permissions concerning marriage as well as concerning the rest of human action and works, and to know which and what sorts of acts have to be done or omitted licitly in accordance with the aforementioned law. Thus, if there is uncertainty or there is a question about whether the incapacity

[*impotentia*] of one spouse to render carnal duties to his or her marital partner is sufficient grounds for performing the licit dissolution of a marriage in accordance with divine law, the servants or teachers of the Holy Scripture mentioned above have to judge and respond to this matter, since as we have frequently said, this duty is theirs. Indeed, by not doing this, they would be punished by the coercive judge according to divine law, although in the future world, not in this one; for this reason, the Apostle says: 'Woe to me if I should not preach the Gospel, for necessity presses down on me' [I Corinthians 9:16].

[2] But suppose there was uncertainty or there was a question about whether such a defect, on account of which a licit dissolution can and ought to be performed, exists in one spouse. Perhaps the spouse who is not suffering from a defect reveals an incapacity or defect suffered by the other spouse and wishes to be separated from marriage because of it, yet it is said not to exist by his or her own spouse or partner. Christ or God has the authority and coercive judgement with regard to this case according to divine law in order to restrain the unjust spouse by punishment in the future world, yet not in this one. For if one spouse would not permit the other the freedom to act justly, but instead inflicts violence upon the person or property of the other, that individual is to be held back, impeded and constrained. Nor, in regard to this, would this judge have to be informed by witnesses in order to know whether such a defect in the other spouse does or does not exist, on account of which one might be separated from marriage, since nothing is hidden from His eyes, as was said earlier.

[3] In accordance with human law, this coercive judgement of divorce, to be imposed upon transgressors by means of enforcement in the present world, pertains to the governors authorized by human law. For although it does not pertain to the human legislator or its coercive law courts to establish or erect spiritual or divine precepts, prohibitions or permissions or counsels, still with regard to human acts connected to these as well as to temporal affairs done or omitted licitly or illicitly by priests who minister to spiritual cares as well as by laymen or secular persons, it pertains to the aforementioned human legislator and judges to determine coercive judgements and to restrain by punishment in the present world those committing illicit acts, since this is not essentially a spiritual matter. For this reason, the Apostle, generally exempting no malefactor or transgressor of those human laws which are not inconsistent with divine laws, says in Romans 13[:1]: 'Everyone is to be subject to the higher

powers', namely kings, governors and tribunes, according to the exposition of the same text by the saint. And he adds: 'For he who resists the powerful resists what God ordains; and he who resists Him secures his own damnation' [Romans 13:2], namely, in eternity. And once again, he says: 'He is a minister of God, avenger in wrath upon him who does evil' [Romans 13:4], which is supplemented by the remark: 'for the sword is not borne without reason', that is, he has weapons or coercive force, which the Apostle says about no spiritual minister, but rather the opposite, when he states: 'The weapons of our soldiers are not carnal' [II Corinthians 10:4]. And once again he says in [II] Timothy [12:4]: 'No soldier of God involves himself in secular affairs', that is, civil litigation. This is also attested by Saint Peter in his Letters, in so far as he says to everyone indifferently, exempting no one: 'For the sake of God, subject yourselves to all human creatures', namely, to constituted governments, 'for example, to the king as the supreme ruler, and to the governors as his agents for the avenging of evil-doers and the praise of the good, since this is the will of God' [I Peter 2:13–14]. In this way, therefore, with regard to marriage and other spiritual affairs which, on their own account or on account of human action concerning them or in connection with them under certain conditions, are related to the statutes of human law made with regard to them (statutes, I say, which are not inconsistent with divine laws, but rather are consonant with and steeped in them), it is appropriate for the coercive secular legislator and judges to determine and judge. Indeed, this may be considered necessary, since in connection with a marriage to be contracted or already contracted many things happen which can be licitly or illicitly done or omitted by human action in regard to which the human legislator ought to regulate and by its authority coercive judges ought to restrain transgressors by punishment. One may propose an imaginary legal suit of this sort, for example, that one or the other spouse, after receiving a judgement regarding the rendering of a dissolution of the marriage between them, did not wish to depart from the other spouse, but to detain that person with himself or herself by force, and also to handle that person and his or her goods and possessions just as these had been handled during the marriage or before its dissolution was rendered by judgement. They are to be punished and coerced by the punishment of the person and his or her property in the present world, and by a coercive judge, in as much as the judgement or sentence had not been observed. For in fact men are permitted certain things with regard and in connection to a female spouse, administering their persons and possessions before a divorce between them is decreed, which are not permitted to them after a divorce, for example, censuring a spouse who is separated from the marriage, assailing and reproving her by abusive words, exacting carnal obligations from her, or treating her shamelessly in some other corporeal manner by beating or whipping her, or attempting to dispose of her dowry or other possessions contrary to her consent, and other similar acts. From this, many and ruinous scandals would probably arise, on account of which such things can and should be done away with and prohibited. For the sake of the clear and common utility – indeed, out of necessity – the human legislator can and should determine, judge and also compel with regard to such deeds and omissions, namely, by assembling the disputants and litigants in court, likewise calling witnesses in order to report the truth, and restraining by punishment those who are unwilling in order that they might appear, and finally, also pronouncing judgement regarding whether the dissolution of the marriage is to occur or not. Yet there must be conformity in this with divine law, namely, its precepts or prohibitions, and what is commanded by this judgement may not be inconsistent with it. Furthermore, both of the disputants or litigants in the court case are to be compelled after receiving the sentence to be obligated by or observant of the judgement, with transgressors against the sentence to be burdened by punishment in the present world. For the divine law has not ordained or established anything in regard to the aforementioned correction or regulation to be inflicted upon transgressors by punishment in the present world, nor has the coercive judge in accordance with it mandated or determined anything at all for the exercise of coercive judgement against any transgressor in the present world, either by Himself or by any one of His successors, whether bishops or presbyters or spiritual ministers, whether communally or separately.

[4] Nor can it be inferred consequentially from this that divine law or its legislator is subject to human law, but rather the converse is the case. For the human legislator prescribes nothing in regard to what is appointed or established by the divine legislator or divine law, nor likewise by its coercive judge, namely, Christ, but rather the reverse is true. Yet the human legislator prescribes and can prescribe justly, and the ministers of the divine law and the remaining laymen are to be constrained by the judges and rulers authorized by it, while doing nothing illicit in connection with or in regard to spiritual affairs. And also it is permitted to and binding upon the same people to exercise their

duties in regard to and in connection with such affairs, and to constrain reasonably by punishment of persons or their property if there were to be transgressions of those precepts of human law which are not inconsistent with the precepts of divine law. For on the basis of the commission of their offices according to divine law and also human precept, bishops or presbyters are bound to teach, to preach and to administer the spiritual affairs of those faithful to Christ, such as baptism and other similar functions. For on account of this, physical or temporal goods are furnished to them by faithful Christians. For this reason, Christ says: 'A worker is deserving of his sustenance' [Matthew 10:10]; and the Apostle says in I Corinthians 9[:11]: 'If we have sown our spiritual seeds among you, is it too costly if we harvest your physical or temporal goods?' On account of this, like workers who receive or may receive a wage, they are obligated and bound, and also can be restrained, by punishment in the present world and by human coercive judges, for the sake of teaching and administering spiritual affairs in a timely and dutiful manner.

[5] But some people say that it follows from the preceding that divine and human law do not differ, since law is a coercive precept, etc., or a collection of such precepts. Therefore, because some precepts of both are identical, the positive as well as the negative ones, for instance, of returning a loan or deposit, not committing theft or robbery, and also other similar acts, it follows that the aforementioned laws are identical. We say, however, that the precepts, actively speaking, of the laws already mentioned are not the same, although they are similar, but they differ in accordance with all the types of causality. First, they differ in their efficient cause, for the precepts of divine law are produced immediately by God, whereas human laws are generated from the minds of human beings or their election and will. Moreover, the final cause of the precepts of divine law is the eternal happiness of human beings in the future world, while the final cause of human law is the tranquillity and finite happiness of this world. The precepts about which we have spoken also differ in material cause: in one case, human beings are the material at hand, in so far as humans are capable of eternal happiness, namely, disposed by faith in Christ, charity, hope and the rest of the virtues. But the material at hand of human precepts is human beings in so far as they are disposed and affected towards tranquillity and power and many other [earthly] things. Finally, the precepts of divine and human law both set out earlier differ in species, or formally, although they may seem similar in genus, just as with the motion of the heavens and the circular

movement of a mill wheel, where one is perpetual whereas the other is not, and just as with the vastness or physical extension of the heavens and the corruptible elements and mixtures, where the one admits of division and the other does not; yet although these are similar or in the same genus, still their atoms are at any rate different formally or in species. Some people have objected to the preceding that the divine legislator has established punishments for transgressors in accordance with His laws in the present world, namely, the imposition of excommunication, which is a punishment in this world on account of transgressions of divine law frequently inflicted on sinners by His command.

[6] We say, however, on the basis of what has been set forth by us in this tract, that excommunication, because it indicates deprivation from civil association, is a punishment of human law, namely, a certain sort of exile, from which follows punishment of property as well as persons, nor is it prescribed by divine law such that punishment is to be inflicted on some sinner. But in reality excommunication, in accordance with what was indicated about the avoidance of certain guilty persons, in regard to their company and society in conversation and discussion, especially in those matters which pertain to the Christian faith and divine worship, is not a punishment of persons or their property, but is a sort of shame and disgrace. On account of this no one is to be deprived of his civil comforts in relation to his person or property by a precept of divine law. For although divine law counsels the avoidance of guilty persons in the manner set forth above, still it does not prescribe avoiding and not associating with them in regard to civil comforts and associations, such as by purchasing bread, wine, meat, fish, pots or clothes from them, if they abound in such items and others of the faithful lack them. This is likewise also true of the rest of the functions and comforts to which they might possibly be judged susceptible in connection with their positions or civil duties and services. For otherwise this punishment would redound in like fashion or for the most part to innocent believers, which was probably not intended by divine law nor by its legislator. Once again, one can perhaps most appropriately say that this avoidance is a counsel rather than a precept.

[7] It is furthermore the case that, should there be such a precept regarding the avoidance of guilty persons, comparable to other precepts of the Scriptures, we would say that it is not a precept for the sake of compelling certain people by punishment of their persons and property in order to prevent the guilty person from association in this way by

means of the imposition of punishments on property and persons in the present world. Consequently, no one is granted coercive power or authority by divine law to restrain guilty persons in the way mentioned before in the present world nor to constrain those who maintain any sort of association, and especially civil association, with them.

[8] Furthermore, if any divine law whatsoever should have conceded such authority and should have granted coercive power in the present world, it may still be said that this was not conceded solely to a presbyter or bishop or the other ministers of spiritual affairs, either communally or separately. On the contrary, the counsel or precept of interdiction was conceded to the church, that is, to the community of those who believe in and appeal to the name of Christ within that locale or region of believers in which and by whom guilty persons ought to be excommunicated or avoided. For this reason, Christ says: 'If your brother has sinned before you', that is, known by you alone, etc.; 'because if he will not heed you nor the witnesses', namely, be corrected by them, 'tell the church, which if he does not heed it', hence, after the judgement of the church, 'he will be to you as a heathen and a tax collector' [Matthew 18:15, 17]. Nor is any statement to be found in Scripture that says: 'Tell only the priests or presbyters or their single assembly', as we have carefully demonstrated above. Consequently, the Apostle says: 'The heretical man is to be shunned after a first and a second admonition' [Titus 3:10], and he did not say to Timothy [*sic*]: 'Are to be coerced or incarcerated', because he was well aware that it did not pertain to his authority at all to coerce anyone by punishment. For from the time of Christ up until the time of the Roman Emperor Constantine I, it is generally agreed that heretics were never coerced or separated from the civil community. Once again, some people may object against the foregoing, saying that human laws are in many cases inconsistent with divine laws. For divine law prescribes certain things which are to be done or omitted in conformity with it but which human law does not prescribe to be done or omitted in conformity with it, such as fornication between unmarried persons or usury or certain other acts which divine law prohibits, yet which human law does not prohibit.

[9] We say, however, that no sort of inconsistency between human and divine law is demonstrated as a result. For Peter to run, and James not to run, is not inconsistent. But if something to be done were prescribed by human law which divine law would prescribe not to be done, the aforementioned precepts would be truly inconsistent, in which case, as

we have said above, divine law and not human precepts are to be followed or obeyed. It is expedient to turn attention to a certain sort of consequence of the foregoing, namely, whether marriage, according to the distinction set forth earlier, is spiritual or not. Marriage seems to some people to be a spiritual matter, since the Apostle, after mention is made of it, says: 'For this is a great sacrament, I say also in Christ and in the church' [Ephesians 5:32], although it still does not seem to be so to other people. For in accordance with the definition already stated, there were valid marriages between infidels, since the Apostle says that 'an unbelieving man is frequently saved by a faithful wife' [I Corinthians 7:14], and likewise the converse. Once again, since it seems that there may be a valid marriage as a result of the purely lay words of men and women, it seems that nothing essential is added by a spiritual rite.

[10] We say, however, that a sacrament in accordance with custom or common knowledge is called the sign of or signifies a holy matter. Whenever the preceding name is correctly applied to the signification of the effect or that matter which was spoken of previously, this signifies the first sense of sacrament. Taking sacrament in its second and well-known sense, it denotes certain words or corporeal objects and certain acts or signs whose display or performance is something brought about by God through the intervention of some human servant. In this sense a sacrament, especially marriage, is not essentially a spiritual matter, but it can be called spiritual because it is a sign or representation of a spiritual matter, just as nourishment or urine is said to be healthy not because the essence of health exists in it but because it produces or indicates health. Yet extending the name sacrament to the effect or result which is produced by the aforementioned sign of God, the foregoing sacrament is a spiritual matter according to the common declarations of the saints and learned teachers of Christian law. Therefore, marriage is not essentially a spiritual matter, although it makes visible the signs of spiritual affairs in accordance with Christian law alone. And when the Apostle says regarding marriage: 'for this is a great sacrament', he is to be understood to mean by 'sacrament' the spiritual matter which we have previously called the 'effect' of the sacrament. This is not to be understood in regard to marriage according to the definition already mentioned by us, namely the mutual consent of spouses, etc., but with regard to marriage of that sort which has the sign in the way we have said and, it seems to me, this sacred matter is the priesthood. And this is why in his exposition, the Apostle himself added: 'I say also in Christ and in the church', for the

combination of male with female in marriage signifies or represents the union of Christ with the church, according to Christian saints and learned teachers, which is nothing other than the union of Christ and the Christian faith effected by Him in the souls of human beings. This faith, effected with the church as the bride of Christ, makes apparent a truly spiritual matter, for which reason the Apostle says: 'Love your wives as Christ loved the church' [Ephesians 5:25]. One may speak about marriage in this kind of way, regardless of whether it is spiritual or not. Yet no coercive judgement about it pertains to bishops or presbyters, whether communally or separately, but only doctrinal judgements according to the method set forth by us already.

Chapter 16

[1] After this, however, it remains to speak here of a related matter and a problem already set out by us: whether a certain degree of blood relation after the first generation impedes entrance into a licit marriage between people in accordance with divine law or whether impediments arise only from the human legislator or law alone, and finally who is authorized to remove such impediments and to give dispensation to people of such degrees of consanguinity who wish to contract [marriage], or who is authorized to relax the punishments which are incurred for this.

[2] We say that although, according to the Old or Mosaic Law, a certain degree of consanguinity prohibiting entrance into a licit marriage was declared or established, believers in Christ are not at all bound to the observation of this, especially since such a prohibition does not exist in the law of Christ. For this reason, the Apostle says, 'For with a changed priesthood, it is also necessary that a change is made in the law' [Hebrews 7:12]; and once again, he says, 'Freed from the Old Law, we serve law in a new way' [Romans 7:6]. According to Christian law, no degree of blood relation, even between brothers and sisters, prevents an entrance into a licit marriage. For this reason, Augustine in 'The City of God', Book 15, chapter 16, treating of such degrees of blood relations, says that entrance into a licit marriage between persons related by consanguinity is not prohibited by divine law and has not yet been prohibited by human law.[17] By these words, Augustine expresses two judgements: the first, already stated above, is that entrance into a licit marriage between persons connected by blood relations is not prohibited by divine law. He also

makes known a second judgement, namely, that such prohibition of entrance into marriage between blood relatives pertains to the authority of the human legislator or its supreme governor, namely, the Roman ruler. Truth compels us to concede and to admit that the same power also pertains to the Roman bishop who is called pope, along with his coterie of clerics who are named cardinals. For the Roman pope asserts his authority pertaining to the removal of the impediment of a blood relation by means of a dispensation for those connected by blood relations to contract a marriage to one another, and also certain Roman pontiffs have in fact given dispensations for numerous such marriages to be overlooked. For if such a degree of blood relation would impede a licit marriage by precept of divine or Christian law, no man – indeed, not even an angel from heaven – could remove this impediment by some dispensation; Christ testifies to this: 'It is easier for heaven and earth to pass away than for a single detail of the law to vanish' [Luke 16:17]; and once again the same idea is expressed when He says: 'The heavens and the earth will pass away, yet my words endure throughout eternity' [Luke 21:33].

[3] From this, it is clearly evident – and the Roman bishop is compelled to admit and in fact to confirm it – that the degree of blood relation does not impede entrance into marriage by divine law or Christian precept, and that if the degree of blood relation impedes anyone from a licit marriage, then this is done or would be done by a precept or statute of human law. The legal precept or statute to give dispensation in regard to this pertains solely to the authority of the Roman ruler or Emperor. Nor may one object that the foregoing marriage is to be prevented on the basis of divine law because it is morally evil, and consequently it would be a mortal sin, and also likewise those who contract into it are bound to eternal damnation, and consequently dispensation from this pertains solely to ecclesiastical servants, bishops or presbyters. For this argument is casuistic [*rhetoricus apparens*] or sophistic, for it accepts what is false, and it does not proceed syllogistically or conclusively. For it accepts what is false, since the preceding marriage is not morally evil, especially in a certain case, for the Roman bishop himself concedes a case in which it may licitly be entered into. Nor once again is it morally evil in an absolute sense, since it is not undertaken directly out of malice, as in the case of theft and other crimes. Consequently, it is not prohibited by divine law, just as Augustine said; as a result, it does not follow syllogistically nor may it be concluded that

dispensations from such action pertain to any bishop or presbyter whomsoever. This is even the case should such marriage be prohibited absolutely by divine law and under threat of the punishment of eternal damnation, since in regard to this prohibition no human being – indeed, not even an angel from heaven – can dispense or ordain or concede what is done licitly, as is indicated above. For this reason, moreover, in connection with the foregoing, the Apostle, speaking of the precepts or mandates of Holy Scripture, says: 'And if an angel from heaven should preach to you a gospel other than this', that is, contrary to this, 'that has been preached to you, it is anathema' [Galatians 1:8], and for no other reason except because the gospels preached by the Apostle were divine prohibitions or precepts. Once again, since the aforementioned marriage is not morally evil, and is not prohibited according to the Old Law (although sometimes it was or may have been a sort of sin in the Old Law, not because it was directly undertaken in an absolute sense or out of malice or moral evil, but only because it was prohibited by the Law, in the manner of eating the meat of pigs and beasts that do not chew cud), therefore it is a virtual [*effectum*] sin, since it was prohibited by Mosaic Law. Yet it is not a sin because it was morally bad or evil in itself, as for instance are theft, homicide, false testimony, and other such acts which are prohibited by divine and human laws because they are morally bad or evil in themselves and are undertaken directly out of malice.

[4] From everything set forth already, therefore, it should be clearly apparent to anyone who is not corrupted by ignorance, malice or both, that the authority of giving dispensation from and also removing impediments to marriage between people and to people joined by blood relations pertains solely to the authority of the human legislator or wholly to its authorized governor, and by no means to any presbyters or bishops whomsoever, even the Roman bishop who is called pope, whether communally or separately. For they are not in and of themselves human legislators, either communally or separately, except perhaps in so far as they exist as a part of the civil community. Moreover, the authority or power to create or make coercive laws in the present world, or to exercise coercive judgement in accordance with them by the punishment of persons or their property, constraining anyone in the present world for the sake of doing or omitting something, does not pertain to any one bishop or presbyter, nor to a single assembly of them, either communally or separately, according to divine law or its concessions or precepts. Rather they are prohibited from these acts by counsel or precept, and the

authority and coercive power of doing so belongs to the community of citizens or the supreme ruler who is called the Roman Emperor, on the basis of valid human reason and sacred Scripture or divine Christian law, and also the words of the saints who expounded on these, and not least by means of the approved chronicles and histories, as is clearly indicated in *Defensor pacis*, Discourse I, chapters 12, 13, 15 and 17, and in Discourse II, chapters 4, 5, 8, 9, 10, 17, 19, 20, 28, 29 and 30, which can be inspected by those who might be interested in verifying what has already been said by us. With regard to all of these topics and proofs, many more things may be called to mind and explicated in this tract on the basis of the *Defensor pacis major*, by means of necessary consequences as well as deductions, on account of which this succeeding tract is to be entitled the *Defensor minor*. Amen. Praise to God.

Notes

1 St Ambrose, *Sermo contra Auxentium*, chap. 2 (in J. P. Migne, *Patrologia Latina* [hereafter *PL*] [Paris, 1844–64], vol. 16, p. 1,050).

2 This passage in fact appears not in Ambrose but in Peter Lombard's 'Commentary on St Paul', *PL*, vol. 192, pp. 16–17.

3 Peter Lombard, *Sententiarum liber*, Book 4, Distinction 18, chapter 9 (vol. 192, p. 889).

4 Ibid., 4.16.7 (*PL*, vol. 192, p. 888). Peter's own reference to 'Pope Leo' is uncertain.

5 St Augustine, *Sermo* 82 (*De verbis Domini*) (*PL*, vol. 38, pp. 508–11).

6 Peter Lombard, *Sententiarum liber*, 4.18.7 (*PL*, vol. 192, p. 888).

7 The first part of the quotation comes from *S. Prosperi Aquitani Sententiarum ex operibus delibatarum S. Augustine*, Book I, chap. 185 (*PL*, vol. 51, p. 453); the second section seems to be loosely based on Prosper, *De vocatione omnium gentium*, Book II, chap. 37 (*PL*, vol. 51, p. 722) [a work whose authenticity has been questioned].

8 St Augustine, *Sermo* 69 (*De verbis Evangelii Matthaei*) (*PL*, vol. 38, p. 441).

9 Pseudo-Isidore, *Decretales Anacleti* (2), chap. 24 (ed. P. Hinschius, *System des Katholischen Kirchenrechts* (Berlin, 1867–69), p. 79.

10 Neither this quotation, nor anything resembling it, appears in Ambrose's commentary on the passage in question, but it does contain echoes of Peter Lombard's comments about the same passage (*PL*, vol. 191, p. 1,040).

11 Aristotle, *Nicomachean Ethics*, 1.3, 1094b27–28 (ed. R. A. Gauthier, *Aristotelis Latinus* (Leiden, 1974), vol. 26, pt. 2).

12 St Bernard of Clairvaux, *De consideratione*, 2.6.10 (*PL*, vol. 182, p. 740).

13 Again, this quote is not to be found in St Ambrose's commentary on the passage in question, but instead seems to derive from Peter Lombard's commentary on St Paul (*PL*, vol. 192, pp. 16–17).

14 St John Chrysostom, *De sacerdotio*, Book 1, part 3 (ed. B. de Montfaucon, (Paris, 1718), vol. 1, p. 374).

15 Hugh of St Victor, *De sacramentis*, Book 2, Part 2, chap. 7 (*PL*, vol. 176, p. 420).

16 Chrysostom, *De sacerdotio*, 2.4 (ed. Montfaucon, vol. 1, p. 375).

17 St Augustine, *De civitas dei*, Book 15, chap. 16 (*PL*, vol. 41, pp. 458–9).

De translatione Imperii
[On the Transfer of the Empire]
(translated by Fiona Watson and Cary J. Nederman)

There are twelve chapters in this treatise. The first concerns the purpose of the narrative. The second shows how the Roman Empire had remained based through the reigns of thirty-three emperors and for 345 years and five months invariably at Rome. The third demonstrates how the peoples of the East, namely, the Persians, Arabs, Chaldeans and other bordering nations, fell from the control of the Roman Empire. The fourth identifies the principal peoples who in the circumstances already described raised rebellion of this kind. The fifth treats the beginning and ordering of the transfer of the control of the Empire from the Greeks to the Franks. The sixth explains how Pepin was elevated, in the time of Zacharias, the Pope at Rome, from master of the palace to King of the Franks. The seventh relates how Pepin, King of the Franks, at the petitioning of the Roman church, marched to Italy against Astulphus, King of the Lombards, defeated him, and restored the temporal possessions of the Roman church. The eighth, how in the time of Pope Adrian, Charlemagne was made Patrician of the city and was granted the administration of the apostolic seat at Rome. The ninth, how the transfer of control of the Roman Empire from the Greeks to the Franks was effected. The tenth, how control of the Roman Empire was transferred from the Franks or Gauls to the Germans. The eleventh, how German electors of the imperial commander were set up. The twelfth is the epilogue of the tract.

Chapter 1

In that treatise which we composed called *Defensor pacis*, we spoke of the establishment of the Roman, and every other, government and of new transfers of power, or any other changes relating to the government, showing how they should and can be achieved rightfully [*de jure*] and in accordance with reason. We now wish to sum up the essay 'On the Transfer of the Seat of Empire',[1] diligently collated from certain chronicles and histories by the venerable Landolph of Colonna, a Roman satrap, whose writing differs in some respects from my own opinion, especially in those cases in which he has interpreted the rights of the Empire according to his own opinion without sufficient proof.

First, then, I shall deal with the transfer of the seat of imperial Rome, by means of which person or persons, and in what manner, it actually passed from the Romans to the Greeks, then from the Greeks to the Gauls or Franks, and most recently from the Franks or Gauls to the Germans.

Beforehand, however, it is necessary to note that, in one meaning, the term 'Roman Empire' [*Imperium Romanum*] sometimes signifies the monarchy or royal rule only of the city of Rome or the Roman civic body [*civitatis*], such as was the case at its origins, as will become plain from what follows.

In another sense, 'Roman Empire' signifies a universal or general monarchy over the whole world, or at any rate over the majority of the provinces, such as was the government and city of Rome as these emerged; it is in accordance with such a meaning that we propose to treat the matter of transfer.

Therefore, beginning in correct order with the earliest events, we will first relate the origin of the city or civic body of Rome and the humble beginnings of its monarchy, then its growth or progress into monarchy over the whole world or the supreme government. Then we will relate its transfer from seat to seat, or from nation [*gente*] to nation in successive periods. What shall be said about the origins and early construction of the city of Rome, let us take from the approved histories.[2] These tell us that Aeneas, a fugitive after the destruction of the mighty city of Troy, travelled to Italy by sea and there founded the Roman Empire, namely, in the place where Rome now is, and sowed the seeds of the Roman nation in that place because it pleased him. This seed, they say, growing in the fullness of time into a most excellent plant, spread its branches over all regions of the earth, like a grain of mustard which from tiny beginnings grows up in wondrous fashion above all herbs, and under its shade all the kings, princes and tyrants of the age with all their peoples relax and enjoy the blessings of peace.

For the Romans, who were descended from Aeneas, managed to subject the world to their command by the exercise of arms, camp discipline, military practice, peaceful liberty, the cultivation of justice, reverence for laws, alliances with neighbouring nations, mature counsel, and dignified speech and action. For the Roman people for 700 years, from the reign of Romulus to that of Augustus Caesar, sent their armies all over the world with such courage and might and crushed all the kingdoms of the world by their strength, that those who read of their magnificent achievements would seem to read of the deeds not of one people but of the entire human race, so that they believe that human fortitude and luck contended with each other to establish their empire.

Chapter 2

According to some, the Roman Empire took its beginnings from Julius Caesar, but more truly from Octavian Augustus, the first Emperor of the Romans. For, according to true history, although Julius Caesar was the first who seized for himself the monarchy of Rome, he was not an emperor but rather a violator and usurper of the republic; and therefore he does not have a place in the litany of the Roman Emperors.

However, the imperial power [*imperium*] remained at Rome without being moved through the reigns of thirty-three emperors and for 354 years and five months, right up until the time of Constantine the Great. Constantine, in the seventh year of his reign, changed the imperial capital, transferring it to the East, to the city of Byzantium which is now called Constantinople and which in accordance with the Empire's laws enjoys the prerogative of ancient Rome. There Constantine established the imperial seat, and he entrusted the administration of Rome, along with certain Italian provinces, to Saint Sylvester, at that time the Roman pontiff, and to his successors, as is related in some histories. At the urging of Saint Sylvester he is also said to have conferred on clerics of the city of Rome certain senatorial honours, mentioned in the history already cited.

These persons, who were then called clerics of the Roman church, are now called cardinals, but before Sylvester were called simply clerics or priests of the Roman church. They did not then have titles referring to their honour and rank but to their work, that is to say, to their duties of preaching, burying martyrs, baptising, and hearing confessions.

These titles were introduced long before Sylvester, in the times of Cletus and Anacletus, Dionysius and Marcellinus. But in the time of Sylvester they received a title benefiting their rank, and that prerogative and honour which the Senate had in the time of Constantine. Anyone who reads our *Defensor pacis* will see whether this was well done or not. Along with these matters, it must be noted that Martinus Polonus in his chronicle gives the number of cardinals, saying that there are fifty-two, that is to say, six bishops, twenty-eight presbyters and eighteen deacons.[3] Some of these are seated by the supreme pontiff, such as the bishops, who sit beside the lord pope during rites and use the episcopal seat.

Some are assistants to the pope, such as the presbyters who assist the lord pope each week during the celebration of Mass and the Hours. Again some are performers of certain duties, such as the deacons; for they perform the ministerial offices. For it is they who clothe the pope and minister to him around the altar. After the bestowing of titles, however, first by Cletus, later by Anacletus and after that by Marcellinus, we find more cardinals, but this does not concern us here.

The historians agree that it was Sylvester who first called these clerics 'cardinals'. For previously, as I have already stated, they were called presbyters of the city of Rome, as is made clear by the 'Ecclesiastical History' of Eusebius,[4] and also by what is said of Novatinus, presbyter of the church of Rome, who, aspiring to the supreme pontificate, tried to hinder the ascension of Pope Cornelius.

Chapter 3

Constantine and the Roman Emperors who succeeded him also held the East under peaceful lordship until the twentieth year of the reign of the Emperor Heraclius, when all the peoples of the East seceded from the lordship of the Latins. But since the reason on account of which they seceded and the manner in which they seceded are not generally known, I have judged it suitable to describe how and why the peoples of the East separated themselves altogether from the Greeks and Latins, in lordship and in worship. The reason why the Easterners, namely, the Persians,

Arabs, Chaldeans and other bordering nations, departed from the sway of the Roman Empire was the tyrannical government of Heraclius.

For after his great victory over the Persians, Heraclius oppressed the Persians and the other Eastern nations with too savage a rule, because of which they unanimously seized on the opportunity for revolt. But so as to set aside their obedience to the Roman Empire irrevocably, following the advice of Mahomet, who at that time was allied with rich and powerful Persians, they adopted a different religion, so that on account of different beliefs and faiths or sects they would not return to this first lordship from the other one. In this they followed the example of Jeroboam, who converted the ten tribes that followed him to a different religion so that they might not return to their old and rightful allegiance.

The Greeks took the same or similar action, for wishing to be separated from obedience to the Roman church, they adopted a different religion or a different ceremony in their ministration, and so fell knowingly into diverse errors. For all their splendid priests, who defend and foment schisms, are Nestorians or Eutictites or Arians or Jacobites or Hebionites. That, then, is what happened in regard to the peoples and nations of those regions in which the insurrection and disobedience already mentioned occurred. For in order that such insurrection would last they induced their followers to break away and leave not just the Empire but Christianity itself, while accepting certain elements common to the law of Moses and to the Gospel, as is made plain in the Koran.

For this reason, it may be noted that certain heretical sects were very friendly towards Mahomet and the laws of the Saracens, which are based on the Koran, for instance, the Nestorians, whom Mahomet orders to be treated with honour.

For this reason, Richard relates in his chronicles[5] that a certain monk by the name of Sergius, who was a Greek and a Nestorian, gave Mahomet instruction for a long time and hence it arises that the Nestorians have large monasteries under the dominion of the Saracens.

Chapter 4

Now that I have sketched the reason and manner of the departure of the Eastern peoples from the lordship of the Greeks and Latins, let us see who were the principal peoples who for the reasons previously mentioned already raised rebellion. Their boldness did not extend merely to insurrection and disobedience, but in addition they hostiley invaded regions within the Roman Empire and areas close to the Emperor.

Here Richard in his chronicles, Martinus, Isidorus, and Admonius in the fourth book of 'The History of the Franks',[6] agree that the principal race to rise to this audacity came from Arabia and the foot of the Caucasus Mountains. According to Jerome's chronicle,[7] this nation is called Nabathean after Nabaoth, the eldest son of Ishmael. Hence they ought to be called not the Saracens but the Agareni or Ishmaelites.

This tribe ravaged parts of the Empire, penetrating as far as Syria and Judaea. The Emperor Heraclius sent out an innumerable army against them which was totally massacred by the enemy, and 150,000 men from the imperial army were slaughtered. Nevertheless, it may be said that the enemy was humanitarian enough to return all the spoils by ambassadors to the Emperor.

Heraclius, however, refused these and procured the aid of the Alani, who are said to have withdrawn from the Caspian Mountains where, it is related, they were confined by Alexander [the Great]. He recruited a new army and gathered an infinite host of soldiers. Two generals led the Saracens and they marshalled 200,000 soldiers for battle. When the two armies, drawn up in readiness for battle, were able to view each other at close range, 5,002 soldiers in the Greek camp were found dead in their beds on the night which would have preceded the day of battle. Stricken with terror and fear, the rest of the army fled in different directions, leaving the whole of the Empire open to the enemy.

Receiving word of so terrible a calamity, and lacking confidence that he could resist, Heraclius fell sick from grief and, seeming to despair, sank into madness, and according to some historians, he committed the sin of Eutyches and married his sister's daughter, called Martina. Other historians, it is true, inform us that he had committed this sin even before the war.

Following this, the Arab and Nabathean army was increased by reinforcements from different provinces that bordered on their country, that is to say, by the Chaldeans, Amonites and Moabites, with whom Mahomet, who, as Richard relates in his chronicles,[8] was leader of Arabia, allied himself.

This Mahomet – trained, it is said, in magical arts but, as I believe, rather moved by his own sagacity [*prudentia*] – on the pretext of scorn for the Empire, persuaded the above peoples away from their way of life to his own so as to augment his own lordship and duped the people in many ways and turned them from their faith, asserting that they could not maintain their government unless they abandoned the Christian faith and obeyed the teachings of the Moslems. He pretended also that he had some sort of divine gift within him and thus, tricking them by means of certain sleights which he performed for them, he passed for a prophet in the general opinion of the people.

By these tricks, too, he seduced a certain noble and powerful widow called Khadijah from the province of Khurasan, even persuading her to marry him, and through her he became ruler of that region. He also deceived many Jews into believing that he was their Messiah.

By such trickeries, by his own power, by a loosening of the law concerning matters of sexual desire, and by promising much for the future, he seduced nations and by the power of arms compelled them to follow him in his apostasy. For by the law given them by Mahomet, those peoples who had taken up arms against the Empire compelled whatever territories they occupied to follow the law of Mahomet. Those who refused to acknowledge it were handed over to be killed. From Arabia they entered Egypt and led astray the people there, then crossing over to Africa they did likewise. From these they even went to Spain and forced the Spanish to give up their old faith. And thus they have multiplied beyond number, more through warfare than preaching.

Chapter 5

After Heraclius' death and after the Empire's power and domination in the East had crumbled, as we have seen, the Empire's capital remained in Greece, at Byzantium, until the time of Constantine VI and of Leo, his son, and through the reigns of thirty-three emperors, counting Constantine the Great, and for 451 years and two months, including the twenty-three years of the reign of Constantine the Great. For that was how long he survived after the transfer of the seat from Rome to Greece.

During the time of Pope Leo III, the transfer of the Empire from Greece to France was to some extent undertaken. This history of this change is not commonly known, because of differences in historians' accounts. Therefore, since the origin or beginning of this change is unknown, it may be recognized and noted that the first cause of this transfer was a dispute between Emperor Leo III and the Roman church over the veneration of church images.

For Emperor Leo III said that images of Christ and the saints ought not to be venerated at all, because this seemed to be a type of idolatry. But Gregory III, who at that time was the head of the Roman church, asserted that the images of Christ and the saints ought to be venerated.

The Emperor Leo upheld his statement to the extent that he came to Rome from Constantinople and removed and carried off with him all the images of Christ and the saints that he found at Rome and condemned them to be burned, and did burn them.

Because of this, the pontiff Gregory III presumed to excommunicate the Emperor Leo and urged the whole of Apulia and all of Italy and the West to secede from Leo's lordship and withdraw their obedience to him. In these dealings, he did for them all that he could and more than he should have – I know not by what authority, but certainly rashly – he solemnly remitted their taxes and, congregating a synod at Rome, confirmed as doctrine the veneration of sacred images and condemned violators of this creed to excommunication.

At last the said Leo died, still holding to these purposes, and was succeeded by his son, Constantine V, who had the same intentions as his father. Since this emperor gave no support to the Roman church, Pope Stephen II resolved to transfer the Roman Empire to some extent from Greece to the Franks. This was in the lifetime of Pepin, who not long afterwards became King of the Franks and who survived that pontiff. Therefore, when some say that the Roman Empire was transferred from Greece to France in the time of this Stephen, it should be understood that a transfer of this kind was ordained during this time but not accomplished in deed. In the time of Pope Stephen, then, a transfer of the Roman Empire to the Franks was ordained, and the Roman clergy were already well acquainted with the favours and kindnesses of the Franks.

Chapter 6

Pepin, son of Charles Martel, a man mighty in war, holding to orthodox doctrines and exceptional in the rectitude of all his ways, is said to have been elevated by Pope Zacharias from major domo to suzerainty in the Kingdom of the Franks, according to the writings of clerics who usurp for themselves an authority belonging to others.

This Zacharias, it is said, deposed the King of the Franks, Childeric, from the kingship, not so much for his vices as because he was too weak to wield such great power, replaced him with the already mentioned Pepin, father of Charlemagne, and absolved all the Franks from their oath of loyalty, by which they were bound to Childeric. But Admonius in his 'History of the Franks'[9] writes more correctly that Pepin was lawfully elected King by the Franks, raised to that position by the princes of the realm and also anointed by Boniface, Archbishop of Rheims, at Soissons in the monastery of Saint Medard.

Childeric, at that time king in name, who was languishing away from indulgence and sloth, was shorn and became a monk. Thus Zacharias did not depose him. For such deposition of a king and establishment of another for a reasonable cause never pertains only to a single bishop or cleric, or assembly of them, but to all the inhabitants of the region, citizens and nobles, or the greater part [*valentior pars*] of them, as I pointed out and showed in my *Defensor pacis*, Discourse I, chapters 12, 13, 15 and 18.

And so we must accept what Admonius says as the truth but reject the writings of the clerics on this matter as prejudiced against the Franks and false. But so that it may become clear why, wherefore and how the transfer of the Empire from Greece to France came about let us briefly pursue the history of this Pepin, King of France and Germany.

Chapter 7

On the death, then, of Pope Zacharias, who had assented to the elevation of Pepin to the throne – although certain sources claim that, even without his assent, Pepin was the rightful King of the Franks – Stephen II, Roman by birth through his father Constantine, attained the supreme pontificate, as we have already seen. According to Admonius, in Book Five of his 'History of the Franks',[10] he was oppressed by Astulphus, King of the Lombards, and came to Pepin in France with a view to recovering the possessions of the church of Rome, of which this Astulphus had despoiled him.

King Pepin travelled three miles to meet him with due ceremony, and conducted him to his royal palace. Then the pope explained in detail to the king the reason for his coming and described at considerable length the injuries dealt to him by Astulphus. Wishing to be of service to him and to carry out his wishes, the king gathered a large army and with the pontiff marched into Italy against Astulphus. Astulphus with all his forces met the king and refused to restore the temporal goods of the Roman church.

Therefore, they entered into battle against each other, in the course of which Astulphus and his forces were defeated, and he was thus compelled to restore the temporal goods of the Roman church. He gave forty hostages from the aristocracy of his realm and promised under oath to restore the possessions of the Roman church.

After these events, Pepin returned jubilantly to France as victor and Pope Stephen returned to his apostolic seat in Rome. Astulphus, however, failed to honour any of his promises to Pepin, and Pepin returned to Lombardy against Astulphus, laid siege to him in Pavia and forced him to fulfil his promises. Then Pepin marched against Ravenna and seized it, and he successfully subdued the entire Pentapolis of the Romagna along with the Exarchate which encompasses Bologna. All of these territories he in effect gave to the church of Rome.

Enticed by these favours and observing the feebleness of the emperor of that time, Pope Stephen, with the aid of his confederates, procured the transfer of the Roman Empire from the Greeks to the Franks, never recalling the favours conceded to the church of Rome by the emperors, but striving to effect the transfer of the Empire to a foreign and distant people, so that, with the Greeks crushed and the Gauls caring little about these matters, he might have a freer reign over Italy.

Therefore, all the writings which state that the Empire was transferred from the Greeks to the Franks in the time of this Pope Stephen ought to be understood in the sense that it was in his time that the transfer was ordained. For it was in the reigns of the next pope and of Leo III that such a transfer was made a reality, as will be seen from what follows.

Chapter 8

And so at the death of this pontiff, Stephen II, the church of Rome was under the protection of Pepin. When Pepin, in the eighteenth year of his reign, went the way of all flesh, his son, called Charles the Great [Charlemagne] by reason of the greatness of his virtues, succeeded his father. After Stephen, there followed three popes whose election and lives I shall pass over. These were Paul I, Constantine II and Stephen III.

Adrian I, a Roman by birth through his father Theodore, and a native of the region of the Via Lata, in the year of our Lord Christ 795 and in the 1,547th year after the founding of Rome, was elected to the supreme pontificate and governed the church of Rome for twenty-three years, ten months and eighteen days. This pontiff entreated Charlemagne, who at that time, as mentioned before, ruled France and Germany, to come to the aid of the church of Rome against the Lombards. For at the death of Astulphus, King of the Lombards, there succeeded him as king his son Desiderius, who, following in the footsteps of his father, despoiled the church of Rome, attaching to himself the houses, cities, castles and the rest of the temporal goods of the Roman church, and oppressing the Romans also with the imposition of tribute and taxes.

For this reason Adrian sent a legate to France, the cardinal and presbyter Peter, imploring the aforementioned Charlemagne for aid [*auxillium*] against Desiderius. The ruler received the legate graciously and, having called a council of lords and prelates, decided to assent to the request of Adrian. Therefore, when this legate had been sent back having obtained the support for which Adrian had hoped, the king prepared a large army and led it, not without considerable difficulties, across the sea and mountain ranges into Lombardy. Arriving in Liguria and Emilia, which is now called the Lombard plain, he set up his tents so that they encircled the city of Pavia and, disposing his camp all around it, he celebrated Christmas there, if the story is to be believed.

At last, leaving his army behind, he went to Rome to worship. There at the same time he celebrated Easter along with Adrian, and when the rites of Easter had been observed he returned to the camp around Pavia. He continued the siege and overcame the city by storming it. He received Desiderius, King of the Lombards, along with his wife and children. Desiderius with his family submitted to the power of Charles. There, too, all the Italian ambassadors and messengers that arrived from individual cities submitted to the power of King Charles. These matters having been settled to his satisfaction, from there he went to Rome and restored the temporal goods of the church of Rome and, out of his generosity, he made at the same time a *de facto* gift of the duchies of Spoleto and Benevento.

Then the Pontiff Adrian, swayed by these generous acts of the king, called together a council of 153 bishops and abbots at Rome. There he and the whole synod gave to the glorious king, Charles, the right and power to choose the Roman Pontiff and ordain the apostolic seat. He then bestowed the dignity of the patriciate on him who had once seemed like a father to the king.

In addition he decreed that the bishops and archbishops of each province should receive their investiture from him. And so that unless a bishop be acclaimed and invested by the king he might be consecrated by none, he anathematized all those who might act contrary to this, and ordered that unless they came to their senses their goods would be given over to the public treasury [*publicare*]. But this pontiff had no authority to grant or do any of these things, nor had any other bishop or cleric, except perhaps only by the ordination and mandate of the Roman people.

Charles is not recorded to have used the first of these rights granted to him, that is to say, the right of appointing the Roman pontiff and deciding the apostolic seat. The reason for this was perhaps that during his reign, from the time this right was granted him, which was a period of forty years, there were few popes. For Adrian and Leo III were the only popes in this space of time, and for forty-four years and several months they were at the head of the Roman church. But not even Charles himself is found by anyone to have renounced the granting of such a right to himself or to have given it up.

Of the second right granted him, that is to say, the installation of bishops, he availed himself several times, as appears in many places in his biography. However, Louis, as it is said, did renounce these rights. But so that we may pursue with more speed our intention of writing about the transfer of the Empire, let us pass over many of the great achievements of Charles.

Chapter 9

At the death, then, of Adrian and in the reign of Charlemagne, defender of the church of Rome, Leo III, Roman by birth through his father Astulphus, was elevated to the office of Roman pontiff. In the year of Our Lord 819 and in the year 1571 from the founding of Rome, this pontiff was made prisoner in Litania, and in Rome was blinded and had his tongue cut out. Though he had been placed under guard he escaped over the wall and took refuge with the legates of Charlemagne, the abbot Guiraud and Winichis, Duke of Spoleto, in whom he had great trust.

This pontiff, as Richard writes in his chronicles,[11] and as some other histories tell – and he who wishes can believe it, because no authentic evidence that he led so saintly a life may be found – had the members which he had lost, that is to say, his eyes and tongue, restored to him in full by divine grace, or so the historians say. He then went to Charlemagne in France, considering him the greatest protector of the church. Charles received him with due honour and, setting out for Rome with him, avenged the wrong done to the pontiff and to the church of Rome, restoring justice.

Admonius also, dealing with these matters more fully in his 'History of the Franks',[12] says that after the king had approached the place which is called Mentana, twelve miles from Rome, Pope Leo, who had preceded the king there, met him with a great escort and, since Charlemagne was the Patrician of Rome, received him with the utmost humility and with every honour, dining with him there (to use the words of the history). Pope Leo and his retinue at once preceded him to Rome. On the next day, too, the pope stood on the steps of the Basilica of Saint Peter the Apostle, having sent out the standards of the city of Rome to meet Charles and having had bands of as many foreigners as citizens disposed in due order in suitable places to acclaim the coming of the king with praise.

He himself with his clergy and bishops welcomed the king as he descended from his horse and ascended the stairs. After making a speech, he presented to him, in the Basilica of Saint Peter, the whole of the Psalms. This was done in the thirty-third year of the king. In addition, after seven days had passed the king made a speech and explained to all why he had come to Rome. He then turned his attention each day to accomplishing those tasks which had brought him to Rome.

However serious the charges made against the supreme pontiff, still, because there was no lawful examiner, the same supreme pontiff, in the presence of all the people and with the approval of the king, ascended, carrying the gospel, the pulpit in the Basilica of Saint Peter and, invoking the name of the Holy Trinity, cleared himself with an oath of the charges laid against him.

Other histories add, in fact, that three cardinals, placing their hands on top of the gospels, declared that all the charges which had been made against the supreme pontiff were false. This clearing of his name was solemnly approved by the whole clergy and confirmed legally by the king.

On the same day, as Admonius writes in his 'History of the Franks',[13] a certain abbot called Zacharias came to Rome with two monks, one from the Mount of Olives, the other from Saint Sab in the East. They had been sent there by the Patriarch of Jerusalem. They brought with them the keys to the Lord's Sepulchre and to the place of Calvary and to the city of Jerusalem, along with the standard of Jerusalem.

Charles received them warmly, detained them with him for several days, treating them with kindness and much honour. Then, when several days had passed he sent them back to Palestine with magnificent presents and gifts befitting his royal majesty.

Some histories relate that, stirred by that embassy, the king, in response to the petition of Constantine VI, who was then emperor, sailed over with a large army and recovered all of the Holy Lands, with the assent of the king of the Persians, who at that time ruled Palestine and all of Syria.

Now, too, the celebrated reputation of the glorious King Charles spread over all the East, so that the king of the Persians, who reigned in the East, aspired to win his good will and sent to him, by messengers and ambassadors, expensive gifts.

The ever victorious King Charles, having recovered the Holy Land, returned to Rome by way of Constantinople, and there he, along with Leo, celebrated with pomp the Nativity.

On that famous day of the Nativity of Christ, when the most glorious King Charles, during the mass and before the creed of Saint Peter, had risen devoutly from prayer, Pope Leo, having solemnly made beforehand whatever preparations were necessary for so solemn a rite, placed the imperial crown on his head, and he was acclaimed by the entire Roman people [*populus Romani*] with these words: 'May Heaven grant Charles Augustus, crowned by God, the mighty and peace-bringing emperor, life and victory'.

All the histories mention this coronation by the Pope and the acclamation and praise of the emperor by the people. Afterwards, like the emperors of ancient times, he was venerated by all without exception, and abandoning the title of Patrician, he was called the Emperor Augustus by everyone.

Charlemagne ruled the Roman Empire for fourteen years. He had also ruled, prior to this, the kingdoms of France and Germany for thirty-three years, during which we find him only referred to as King and Patrician. But from the thirty-third year, after his coronation as emperor, all the annals, all the records of his deeds, and all the histories when they refer to him without exception call him the Emperor Augustus.

The extent of the strength, rectitude [*iuris*] and firmness which this transfer of the Empire had is revealed in the final chapter of my *Defensor pacis* and can be clearly perceived by all. This transfer of the Empire from the Greeks to the Franks remained with the Franks through seven generations, namely, the reign of seven emperors, for 103 and more years.

Chapter 10

The Emperor Arnulf, last of the descendants of Charlemagne, was an effeminate and worthless person; he was remiss and timid in opposing the despot Berengar, who was at that time waging war in Italy on the church of Rome, and others who were also attacking it in many regions. Indeed, at that time he was himself persecuting the church at Rome, as Martinus Polonus and Tusencius write.[14]

When the son of this Arnulf, having not yet been consecrated as emperor, was defeated by Berengar, tyrant over Italy, and mutilated at Verona, the line of Charles in the Empire became entirely extinct. Berengar became ruler of Italy and the church of Rome, pressed hard by persecutions, began to totter, first, because this despot was persecuting the church and, second, because not a true shepherd but a mercenary held sway over the church, namely, John, son of Albert (as Sicard, Bishop of Cremona, a great historian, relates). The cardinals, all of one mind, in the year of our Lord 950 wrote to the Duke of Saxony, who wielded great power and ruled all the Allemagne. He was also a devout man, of the Catholic faith, far-sighted in counsel, just in his judgements, faithful in his undertakings, energetic in warfare and distinguished by the integrity of all his ways, showing also his devotion to the Church of God in all his religious observances.

It was from this man, then, that the cardinals implored aid, asking that he protect and assist the Roman church which was tottering under the many kinds of onslaughts made against it. He gathered a great army, crossed over to Italy, engaged Berengar in battle, defeated him and his army, and then slew him.

Soon after this he proceeded to Rome, summoned a council of the cardinals and, realizing from what they told him that the pope was incorrigible, advised him to renounce the papacy. When the pope proved obdurate he shut him up by force in the fortress of Saint Angelo, and compelled him to resign it.

Leo VIII then became the pastor of the church of Rome. Once elected, Leo, because of Otto's championing of the church of Rome (both in taking action concerning Berengar, who had been making trouble for the church, and then in his reformation of the church) granted to Otto the same rank and privileges which Adrian had conferred on Charles. Moreover, he called a synod and before the assembled clergy and people he appointed him Emperor. No election took place before this but forty years later an election was instituted. This was how the transfer of the Empire from the Franks or Gauls to the Germans took place. Otto I ruled the Empire in peace for eight years after his ordination as Emperor. His son and grandson also ruled in succession and uncontested.

Chapter 11

After these events, when Otto III died without sons, Gregory V, of the Teutonic race, and a kinsman of Otto, became the supreme pontiff.

It was in the time of this pontiff that electors of the emperor were first appointed. These were seven German princes, four of them from the laity, and three clerics or prelates, as Martinus records.[15]

For since the three Ottos had succeeded to the Empire by a sort of hereditary right, it was found prudent and expedient for the good order of the Church of God to decree that such unrivalled power, which ought to be the prize of rectitude rather than of birth, should not be passed on by way of succession but of election so that it would be esteemed most worthy of the administration of the Empire.

Therefore, it was instituted that the emperor is to be elected by seven imperial officials of princely rank, after which he is to be crowned with the imperial diadem by the supreme pontiff; these electors include, as mentioned, three prelates, who were and are the chancellors of the emperor. These are: the Archbishop of Cologne, who is chancellor of Italy; the Archbishop of Trier, who is chancellor of Gaul; and the Archbishop of Mainz, who is chancellor of Germany. There are also four barons, who were and are in the service of the Roman emperor. These are the Marquis of Brandenburg, the Duke of Saxony, the Duke of Bavaria and the King of Bohemia. Hence this verse:

> Anyone from Mainz, from Trier or Cologne
> Of the Empire may be chancellor.
> A palatine's waiter; a duke, sword bearer,
> a Marquis, chamberlain; and the butler, the Lord of Bohemia.
> It is these who through the ages decree the supreme Lord.

This arrangement dates back to 1004, as the chronicles of Germany make clear.[16]

Chapter 12

From the preceding narrative, then, it is quite clear that in the time of King Pepin and Stephen, Pope of Rome, a transfer of the Roman Empire from the Greeks to the Franks was ordained, as a result of the previously stated circumstances. In the time of Adrian I, Charlemagne was appointed disposer of the church of Rome, elector of the Roman Pontiff, and Patrician of the city of Rome. In the time of Leo III, Charlemagne was made Emperor of Rome, and it was in his time, too, that the actual transfer of the Empire from the Greek rulers to the Franks occurred.

At last, with the passage of time and the revolution of many years, in the time of Leo VIII, Pope of Rome, the transfer of the Empire from the Frank or Gallic rulers to the Germans took place.

Later, in the time of Gregory V, the election of the Roman Emperor was granted to the seven German princes previously mentioned, who right up to modern times have selected the Roman Emperor, who is crowned by the Bishop of Rome for the sake of ceremony rather than on account of some necessity. This was the manner of the transfer of the Empire to the Teutons or Germans.

These developments were all aims of the bishops of Rome and were accomplished with their assent. What force they had and have today is explained in our *Defensor pacis*, Discourse I, chapters 12 and 13, and in the final chapter of the second discourse, for anyone with a serious interest in the subject.

Here ends the treatise 'On the Transfer of the Empire'.

Notes

1 Landolph of Colonna, *De translatione Imperii* (in M. Goldast, ed., *Monarchia Sancti Romani Imperii*, 3 vols. (Frankfurt, 1611–1614), vol. 2, pp. 88–95).
2 Martinus Polonus, *Chronicon imperatorum et pontificum* (in *Monumenta Germaniae Historica* (Hanover, 1839–1921), *Scriptores*, vol. 22, ed. L. Weiland).
3 Ibid., p. 407.
4 Eusebius of Cesaria, *Ecclesiastica Historia*, trans. St Jerome (in J. P. Migne, *Patrologia Latina* [hereafter *PL*] (Paris, 1844–1864), vol. 19).

5 Richard of Cluny, *Chronicon* (ed. E. Martene and U. Durand, *Veterum Scriptorum et Monumentorum . . . Amplissima collectio* (Paris, 1724–1733), vol. 5, pp. 1158–74).

6 Ibid., chap. 3; Martinus Polonus, *Chronicon imperatorum et pontificum*; Isidore of Seville, *Chronicon maius* (in *PL*, vol. 83, pp. 1,017–58); Admonius of Fleury, *Gesta Francorum*, Book 4, chap. 22 (in *PL*, vol. 138, pp. 627–798).

7 Actually, a reference to Jerome's translation of Eusebius's *Ecclesiastica Historia*, pp. 315–598 and 689–92.

8 Richard of Cluny, *Chronicon*, p. 1161.

9 Actually, the anonymous continuation of the *Gesta Francorum* of Amdonius of Fleury (ed. A. Duchesne, *Historia Francorum Scriptores* (Paris, 1636–1649), vol. 3, pp. 1–20).

10 Ibid., pp. 1–20.

11 Richard of Cluny, *Chronicon*, p. 1,161.

12 Admonius of Fleury, *Gesta Francorum*, Book 4, chap. 89.

13 Ibid., p. 1,162.

14 Martinus Polonus, *Chronicon imperatorum et pontificum*, Book 4, chap. 87.

15 Ibid., Book 4, chap. 148, 90.

16 Ibid., Book 4, chap. 90.

Table of biblical citations

All references are to chapter and section numbers of the *Defensor minor*.

Index of proper names

85

Subject index

aid (*auxillium*), 75
alms-giving, 8, 21–2, 46
apostles of Christ, 8, 30

baptism, 48, 56
binding and loosing of souls, 1, 10–11, 14–15, 20, 29
bishop, 1, 3, 4, 6, 7, 8, 9, 11, 12, 20, 22, 23, 25, 28, 29, 30, 32, 33, 34, 36, 37, 38, 39, 41, 46, 48, 49, 50, 51, 52, 55, 56, 58, 60, 61, 62, 68, 73, 75, 76, 77, 79, 80, 81

Cardinals, College of, 12, 42, 61, 67, 68, 79
cause, 2, 5, 56, 71, 73
Chalcedon, Council of, 41
Christ, dual nature of, 35, 36
church (Roman), 36, 37, 38, 39, 65, 68, 69, 71, 72, 73, 74, 75, 76, 79, 81
Church (universal), 19, 37, 38, 39
citizens, 2, 33, 50, 63, 73, 77
'The City of God' (St Augustine), 60
civic body (*civitas*), 6, 50, 66
civil association, 1, 12, 30, 31, 32, 33, 57, 80
civil community (*universitas civilis*), 2, 19, 39, 50, 58, 62, 63
coercive power, 4, 47, 48, 52, 58, 63
community of the faithful (*universitas fidelis*), 31, 32, 34, 58
confession, 11, 12, 13, 14, 15, 16, 19, 21, 68
consanguinity, 43, 60
consent, 19, 27, 33, 38, 44, 55, 59
Constantinople, Council of, 41

counsel, 13, 16, 20, 22, 23, 24, 25, 28, 29, 34, 44, 45, 46, 53, 57, 58, 62, 67
crusading, 21–2
custom, 37, 38, 43, 52, 59

deacons, 3, 10, 68
Defensor pacis (Marsiglio), 1, 2, 3, 4, 5, 6, 7, 9, 10, 11, 21, 23, 29, 31, 32, 33, 34, 35, 38, 40, 41, 42, 43, 50, 63, 66, 68, 73, 78, 81
deposition of king, 73
De sacrementis (Hugh of St Victor), 49
De verbis Domini (St Augustine), 36
'The Dialogues' (St John Chrysostom), 32
disgrace, 16, 57
disposition (*habitus*), 17, 18, 44
divorce, 43, 52, 53, 54, 55

Eastern Empire, secession of, 68, 69
'Ecclesiastical History' (Eusebius), 68
Electors, Imperial, 65, 80
Ephesus, Council of, 41
Eucharist, 10
excommunication, 1, 7, 12, 29, 30, 31, 32, 33, 57, 58, 72

faith, articles of, 37, 38
fasting, 21, 26, 46
fear, 14, 16, 17, 47, 70
festivals, 21

general council of the church, 18, 19, 21, 26, 37, 38, 39, 41, 42
greater part (*valentior pars*), 2, 6, 33, 34, 39, 41, 50, 73

88

CAMBRIDGE TEXTS IN THE HISTORY OF POLITICAL THOUGHT

Titles published in the series thus far

Aristotle *The Politics* (edited by Stephen Everson)

Arnold *Culture and Anarchy and Other Writings* (edited by Stefan Collini)

Bakunin *Statism and Anarchy* (edited by Marshall Shatz)

Bentham *A Fragment on Government* (introduction by Ross Harrison)

Bernstein *The Preconditions of Socialism* (edited by Henry Tudor)

Bodin *On Sovereignty* (edited by Julian H. Franklin)

Bossuet *Politics Drawn from the Very Words of Holy Scripture* (edited by Patrick Riley)

Burke *Pre-Revolutionary Writings* (edited by Ian Harris)

Cicero *On Duties* (edited by M. T. Griffin and E. M. Atkins)

Constant *Political Writings* (edited by Biancamaria Fontana)

Diderot *Political Writings* (edited by John Hope Mason and Robert Wokler)

The Dutch Revolt (edited by Martin van Gelderen)

Filmer *Patriarcha and Other Writings* (edited by Johann P. Sommerville)

Harrington *A Commonwealth of Oceana* and *A System of Politics* (edited by J. G. A. Pocock)

Hegel *Elements of the Philosophy of Right* (edited by Allen W. Wood and H. B. Nisbet)

Hobbes *Leviathan* (edited by Richard Tuck)

Hooker *Of the Laws of Ecclesiastical Polity* (edited by A. S. McGrade)

John of Salisbury *Policraticus* (edited by Cary Nederman)

Kant *Political Writings* (edited by H. S. Reiss and H. B. Nisbet)

Lawson *Politica sacra et civilis* (edited by Conal Condren)

Leibniz *Political Writings* (edited by Patrick Riley)

Locke *Two Treatises of Government* (edited by Peter Laslett)

Luther and Calvin on Secular Authority (edited by Harro Höpfl)

Machiavelli *The Prince* (edited by Quentin Skinner and Russell Price)

Malthus *An Essay on the Principle of Population* (edited by Donald Winch)

Marsiglio of Padua *Defensor minor* and *De translatione Imperii* (edited by Cary Nederman)

James Mill *Political Writings* (edited by Terence Ball)

J. S. Mill *On Liberty*, with *The Subjection of Women* and *Chapters on Socialism* (edited by Stefan Collini)

Milton *Political Writings* (edited by Martin Dzelzainis)